It is my privilege to have known Donna Wilcox, (formerly Donna Grant) for more than twenty years. Our families have been knit together by a cord of God's love that has weathered the test of time. Bob and Donna Wilcox have been a wonderful part of our church's ministry for several years, serving as Choral Director and Director of World Missions. It has been exciting to see the Lord open doors for them of ministry through World Missions. You will truly be blessed, as we are, to get to know Donna Wilcox through the pages of *Falling into Faith,* and hear the road she has traveled from tragedy to triumph!

Greg Coleman
Senior Pastor
The Harbor at Holley

Writing *Falling into Faith* has been an exercise of love and fun for Donna. To read it is like sitting in the room with its author and hearing her tell the stories, she is so wonderful at telling. She can keep you in stitches one minute and make you want to get down on your knees in prayer the next; all the time she has been witnessing for Christ without you even being aware of it. Her passion, energy, faith in God, love of family, and sense of humor are powerful and can be seen in every page of this book. One would never guess the hardships she has faced, and those same hardships she has put into God's hands, refusing to worry. She has only been in my life for a few years, but what a role model she has been!

Betty Devinney
Retired Business Executive
Former Senior Vice President
Eastman Chemical Company

Donna and I worked at the same Corporation for several years. Her love for Jesus Christ and people is shown daily in the way she always shares a word of encouragement from the Bible. She helped us through some of the most difficult times in our lives and she is the most cheerful witness for Jesus we have ever met. Her constant testimony to others and unshakable faith continues to inspire us in our walk with the Lord. *Falling into Faith* will move and challenge the reader as she shares her incredible testimony!

Linda & Nathan Chessher
Muscogee Nation of Florida
A.K.A. the Florida Tribe
of Eastern Creek Indians

Donna's excitement for life, love for the Lord, and incredible faith is an encouragement to anyone who knows her. Her testimony will strengthen you as you face life's difficult challenges. As you read *Falling into Faith*, get ready to laugh, cry, and fall more into love and faith with the Lord!

Deborah Rajkovich
School of Biblical Studies

falling into

FAITH

falling into

FAITH

Cast your cares on the Lord and He will sustain you;

He will never let the righteous fall. Psalm 55:22

Donna Wilcox

TATE PUBLISHING *& Enterprises*

TATE PUBLISHING
& Enterprises

Scripture quotations marked "KJV" are taken from the *Holy Bible, King James Version*,
Cambridge, 1769.

Scripture quotations marked "NIV" are taken from the *Holy Bible, New International
Version* ®, Copyright © 1973, 1978, 1984 by International Bible Society. Used by
permission of Zondervan Publishing House. All rights reserved.

Scripture quotations marked "TAB" are taken from *The Amplified Bible, Old Testament*,
Copyright © 1965, 1987 by the Zondervan Corporation and *The Amplified New
Testament*, Copyright © 1958, 1987 by The Lockman Foundation. Used by permis-
sion. All rights reserved.

This book is designed to provide accurate and authoritative information with regard
to the subject matter covered. This information is given with the understanding that
neither the author nor Tate Publishing, LLC is engaged in rendering legal, professional advice. Since the details of your situation are fact dependent, you should addi-
tionally seek the services of a competent professional.

Published in the United States of America

ISBN: 978-1-5988676-2-6
12.03.14

DEDICATION

Falling Into Faith is dedicated first and foremost to God who is a powerful and faithful Father, Jesus Christ who shed His blood for our salvation, healing, and so much more, and the ever-present companion and friend, the sweet Holy Spirit.

With heartfelt gratitude, I want to thank the two men who have made my life richer and blessed beyond belief: My loving and supportive husband Bob Wilcox, and my devoted and handsome dad, Rev. Edward Grant.

To Bob, I love you baby! Our years together have been filled with adventure, fun, and so much joy. It is a privilege to be married to someone I respect and admire as much as I do you. Thanks for hanging in there with me through all the long hours of writing, editing, and hearing the same stories over-and-over again. I don't know what God has in store for us next, I am just happy to be with you on this journey. We are so blessed!

To Daddy, I truly love and appreciate you. Thank you for always being there for all of us. You are a friend and father to so many people scattered around the globe. Your spirit of giving has continued to amaze me through the years. I am proud to be your daughter, and I will always be your baby!

A special "I love you" to my stepdaughter, Traci. You are beautiful inside and out and possess wisdom beyond your years. Thank you for allowing me to be a part of your life.

A special thanks to Jeanne Marie, Christian fiction writer and author of "Angel in the Saloon." The enormous amount of time you spent helping me with my manuscript in its beginning stages, offered confirmation and strength when I needed it most. May God bless all the works of your hands!

A special thanks to Shana Keller. Thank you for all the long hours you spent going over my manuscript and making sure I did not miss anything! You are not only amazing but God has given you a precious gift and a powerful testimony of restoration. He *will* fulfill the dreams and purposes He has for your life. Your ability to stand as the *Righteousness of Christ* and hold tight to God's forgiveness has challenged and strengthened my faith in a beautiful way!

A special thanks to all the "spiritual kids" God has brought into our lives. I know you are grown, but you will always be our kids. I wish I could list every name but I pray you all know just how much Dad Bob and Mama Donna love you. Thank you for making our lives richer in ways we never imagined! Continue to grow in God and never forget He has a very special plan for each one of you. When you get lonely or just feel the need to *try* and beat Mama Donna at a game of dominos, Skip Bo, Yahtzee, or 10,000... COME HOME! There will always be a good ole Southern home-cooked meal waiting.

A special thanks to all our family and friends. We love you very much and cannot thank you enough for your prayers, love, and support! Your generosity has allowed us to accomplish many things while on the mission field, as well as working with young missionaries stateside.

Finally, but just as important, I want to thank Tate Publishing Company for allowing me to share my story with the hope of bringing encouragement, *Truth,* and laughter to all who read it.

Bob and Donna Wilcox

Rev. Edward and Mary Grant

CONTENTS

FOREWORD

The Psalmist boldly says, "My soul shall make its boast in the Lord" and that is what my dear friend Donna is doing in her book *Falling Into Faith*. It documents the ability of her God to be her Friend, Lover, Companion, and Guide, as well as her Counselor and her Comforter through the tests, trials, temptations, and the triumphs that have made up her life.

Modern day Christians need to know the God that we read about in the Bible is the same today. He has lost NONE of His ancient power! If only we will put our trust in Him and yield our lives to Him as Donna has done, we too will prove the greatness of His love. Thank you Donna for being so honest in *Falling Into Faith* and drawing our attention not to yourself, but to the God you love and serve.

Reona Joly
Missionary
International Speaker
Author, *Tomorrow You Die*

INTRODUCTION

Falling Into Faith is about an imperfect, but ever growing faith which learns the joy of *falling* into a *trust relationship* with God; knowing He will not allow the righteous to fall (Psalm 55:22). It is also about the power of God in the name of Jesus to heal and restore our lives, even when our faith *feels* weak and inadequate.

God literally brought me back from the brink of death due to sickness and disease. With patience, His love and grace remained constant even when I strayed from His will to choose my own path.

In this ongoing journey, I have experienced what a loving and faithful Father Jesus Christ the Son of God is to ALL who *fall* into His loving hands of mercy, and how He cares for His children without showing favoritism.

As you read the pages of my life, I pray the *eyes of your understanding* are opened to see God as the Loving, Forgiving, and Faithful Father He is. I pray you come to the full knowledge with certainty and without reservation that He is "The God of Restoration." One who longs to bring hope to the hopeless and replace the ashes and ruins of our lives with beauty and abundance. His only requests are *faithful obedience to His Word, to love Him with all your heart, and to love one another.*

I refer to Jesus Christ, God the Father, and the Holy Spirit throughout my book. God is a single being existing simultaneously as three distinct persons. The Bible clearly speaks of God the Father, God the Son (Jesus Christ) and God the Holy Spirit. According to scripture, the three are co-equal and co-eternal, one in essence, nature, power, action, and will.

Obedience to the Holy Spirit is why I have written this book. Stepping out in faith and out of my comfort zone presented many new challenges. The Lord assured me if I simply obeyed, He would equip and perform a new work in my heart and life. Faithful and true to His Word, He continues to fulfill His promise in amazing ways!

There is an old saying, *"blondes have more fun."* Unfortunately, for most of my life this little quip did not apply to me, but I am making up for it now! I may not possess the wisdom and knowledge of Solomon but *I know . . . that I know . . . that I know . . . God is faithful and His Word is Truth. What He has done for me, He promises to do for you too!*

The Word says, *"They overcame him by the blood of the Lamb and by the word of their testimony"* (Revelations 12:11). Because of this, I rejoice in sharing my testimony of healing and restoration. Some things you may find humorous and other things just down right painful! Above all, I pray you are challenged and encouraged.

> So do not be ashamed to testify about our Lord, or ashamed of me his prisoner; But join with me in suffering for the gospel, by the power of God, who has saved us and called us to a holy life—*not because of anything we have done,* but because of *His own purpose and grace.* This grace was given to us in Christ Jesus before the beginning of time.
>
> (2 Timothy 1:8–9 NIV, emphasis added)

> . . . I will instruct thee and teach thee in the way which thou shalt go; I will guide thee with Mine eye.
>
> (Psalm 32:8 KJV)

With Jesus Christ as the Lord of our lives, we have the greatest source of power.

There is none greater! Before beginning this adventure of *falling,* allow me to leave you with a few truths:

*The Truth is...*Christ died for every one of us. He alone has the power to save, heal, and restore!

*The Truth is...*There is forgiveness of sin for *all* who ask in faith and receive through the blood of Jesus!

*The Truth is...*You can break the generational curses of sin and bondage in your life through Christ and His shed blood!

The Truth is... God is victorious and Satan is already defeated!

*The Truth is...*Everything we receive from God is *by faith.*

Therefore, by faith we must be willing to believe and receive!

...and everything that does not come from faith is sin.
(Romans 14:23 NIV)

Now, let's get going. Come travel with me on this roller coaster ride I call my life and have a great time *falling!*

CHAPTER 1

Mischief and Miracles

Born in Mobile, Alabama, I grew up in Fort Walton Beach a small town in sunny Northwest Florida. Miles of beautiful beaches grace the area with sand as white as snow—not a bad place to call home! The youngest of three preacher's kids (commonly referred to as pk's) I proudly wore the title, "baby of the family." Larry was the eldest, eleven years older than me, and my sister Robbie was three years older.

As a young man, my father answered the call to preach. A licensed and ordained Assembly of God Minister, our lives revolved around church. A preacher's home is usually the center of attention and we were no exception to this rule. Too often, it seemed a spotlight shone directly on our house, giving people a lot to observe, judge, gossip, and pray about!

Early on, I faced numerous health problems. Always labeled "the sick one," I desired more than anything to be healthy and strong. Comments like, *"Oh poor Donna, she's so sick"* had a profound and adverse affect on my life, both mentally and physically. Through it all, we still managed to fill our home with many happy memories.

A few years after I was born, Dad took a pastoral position at a church in Graceville, a small town in Florida. We lived in the parsonage located next to the church. The town had a charming Mayberry R.F.D. kind of setting, with a small close-nit community. Only two-years-old at the time, I still vaguely remember our little white house, long front porch, and white picket fence. Directly across the street stood a playground with a small park bench in front, which captivated my attention. Mother kept a watchful eye because she knew her little girl's weakness—socializing! If anyone sat down alone, I wanted to dart across the road with the hope of making a new friend. Mother stated I often begged and pleaded, *"Please Mommy, let me go, they are all alone with no one to talk to."* The ultimate little social bug, I cannot ever remember feeling shy. I truly loved being around people and making friends.

Mother, a talented musician, sang and played the piano, organ, and accordion. She began teaching us to sing as soon as we could talk. God put a song inside my heart at a very young age. By the time I was two, my sister, mother, and I harmonized and sang in church and on the radio. Being so little, Mom often stood me on the altar next to the piano allowing the congregation to hear and see me. She said I loved the attention. Music and people became my passions. Blessed with a good set of lungs, (a nice way of saying I sang loud), I sang anytime, anywhere, and for anyone willing to listen. After all these years Dad still has old cassette tapes of "his girls" singing.

One Sunday morning my parents were getting ready for church. Robbie and I had measles so we stayed home with Larry. Giving in to my pitiful pleas, Mama finally agreed that if Larry stayed right with me I could sit on the bed and cut out paper dolls. Everything seemed to be going along just fine until the phone rang. Larry ran to answer it and for no apparent reason I began jumping on the bed with scissors in my hand. These were not children's scissors; they were the long, sharp, stainless steel kind. I knew this was a big no-no, but kids will be kids!

You can guess what happened next. Falling off the bed, I landed on the scissors stabbing myself in the chest. Hearing the bang, Larry ran back in the room. To his horror he found me face down on the floor and motionless. Turning me over he saw the scissors plunged deep into my chest, with just the handle exposed. Larry yelled for Robbie to run over to the church and get Mom and Dad. Within minutes, they rushed in finding me on the floor in my brother's arms. Panicking, Larry suddenly grabbed the handle and pulled out the scissors but no blood was coming from the wound. Fearing there could be internal bleeding, everyone prayed as Daddy scooped me up in his arms to take me to the nearest hospital in Dothan Alabama, approximately twenty minutes away. The entire congregation and many of our neighbors followed closed behind.

Word quickly spread to the local radio station as people called out in the community for prayer. The disc jockey informed listeners about the accident and asked everyone to pray for "little Donna Grant."

The emergency room doctor took x-rays to determine the severity of the wound. He soon came out in disbelief, advising my parents the scissors literally missed my heart and lungs by a hair, and there appeared to be no trace of internal bleeding. He exclaimed, *"This is nothing less than a miracle!"*

After this incident, people came to our church to see the little girl who had the whole town praying. Mother never wanted us to forget God's hand of protection. She kept the newspaper article in a drawer at home, often reading it as a reminder.

This was only the beginning of the enemy's attempts to destroy my life. The scar remains today along with many others. They serve as a reminder of Satan's failures and God's miracle working power. Father God is our Healer and Protector, and nothing is too hard or impossible for Him!

When we commit our lives to the Lord and walk in obedience, the Bible tells us He will take a curse and bring forth a blessing. When God performs "the miraculous" in our lives it is not solely for our benefit. He can use it to bring salvation, hope, blessing, healing, and wisdom to many hearts and lives.

Throughout the Bible, there are numerous stories of God's amazing power, turning what was meant for evil into something good. The story of Joseph is an excellent example, and his words in the following scripture show a profound wisdom and understanding of God's hand carefully working *"all things for the good."*

> His brothers then came and threw themselves down before him. 'We are your slaves,' they said. But Joseph said to them, "Don't be afraid. Am I in the place of God? You intended to harm me, but God intended it for good to accomplish what is now being done, the saving of many lives. So

then, don't be afraid. I will provide for you and your children." And he reassured them and spoke kindly to them.

(Genesis 50:18–21, NIV)

Although Joseph knew his brothers meant to harm him, he saw how God used his situation to save many lives. His obedience and perseverance saved the Israelites, the Egyptians, and all the nations that came to Egypt to buy food in the face of a famine that threatened the very existence of the known world.

We will discuss the story of Joseph in more detail in the following chapter, however, set aside time to read chapters 37 through 50 in the book of Genesis. It will strengthen your heart and encourage you to trust God in the face of life's struggles and hard circumstances.

Prior to becoming pastors, Mom and Dad were traveling evangelists. They felt a particular burden for a small church in Fort Walton Beach, Florida while holding a revival there several years earlier. A pastoral position became available and although our family loved Graceville, it came time to move on. We said our goodbyes and moved to a place we called home for many years to come.

CHAPTER 2

Devil Possessed Chickens and Bikinis!

Some of my fondest memories as a child were Saturday visitations with my father. One particular Saturday he only had one planned visit, so my parents decided to take us all shopping. On the way, they would make a quick stop to pray for an elderly couple who was sick and unable to get around very well, and then off to town we'd go. Pulling in the drive, Larry requested to stay in the car but Robbie and I wanted to sit on their front porch. Exiting the car, Mom instructed Larry to keep a close eye on us.

Young, gullible, and barely three at the time, my sister could make me believe anything. She convinced me God spoke directly to her, giving specific instructions on things we were suppose to do for Him. It did not matter how strange the request, with all my heart I believed she heard directly from heaven. Once Robbie received one of these "so called revelations," trouble soon followed. The highlight of Larry's existence seemed to be watching the predicaments his little sisters got into due to these "revelations." The fact that I never learned my lesson added to his amusement.

The elderly couple lived in a little white house with a screened in front porch, which ran the full length of the house. An old stove sat by the entrance door filled with bowls full of eggs. In fact, there were **many** bowls of eggs all over the porch because this was their source of income. The yard had a large, fenced-in area with chickens running all around. Some of them were very odd looking with a strange red thing on the tops of their heads. Not knowing they were roosters, I asked my "all knowing" sister, *"Robbie, what's the red thing on those chicken's heads?"* She proceeded to tell me about a message she received straight from heaven, *"Oh Donna, the Lord told me they*

20

are demon possessed chickens, and we are suppose to throw eggs at them and make the red thing fall off to cast the demons out!"

Certain Robbie had heard from God, I began hurling eggs toward those poor roosters. A three-year-old cannot throw very far, and all my eggs ended up on the front sidewalk. As this ritual of exorcism played out, Larry peered from the car in amazement, wondering what in the world his little sisters were thinking and laughing hysterically.

Mom and Dad eventually came out to find us dutifully standing on the porch. They were inside maybe ten minutes, but it does not take children long to get into mischief! Parents often have a sixth sense when it comes to their kids, and something sure didn't seem right. They began noticing the empty bowls. Where were the eggs?

The real *tell all* awaited them outside on the sidewalk. Looking down at all the broken eggshells Mom turned toward us with a glare and in disbelief she asked, *"What have you girls done?"* I immediately knew Robbie must have gotten her information from God all messed up. Surely He wouldn't tell her to do something that would get us in trouble . . . *Big trouble!* Confused and not wanting a spanking, I pointed to the sky and said, *"Mama, you won't believe it but this huge bird flew over and dropped all these eggs!"*

Remorse for telling a lie quickly took over and I blurted out the whole ugly truth. I begged her to understand. We were just trying to cast the devil out of the chickens, but she did not want to hear it. *"Doesn't Mama care about those poor chickens?"* It was then I received an education about roosters! This left me with a perplexing question, *"God made all the animals, so why didn't He tell Robbie about those roosters, and why did He tell her they were demon possessed chickens?"* Somehow, my little brain concluded she did not get the information straight and yet I still believed Robbie had a direct line to God. She told me she did.

Madder and hotter than a firecracker, Mother yelled for Larry as she dragged us to the car. In tears from laughing so hard, Larry explained to Mom and Dad how hilarious the whole thing had been to watch. They tried to hold back, but waves of laughter soon followed. Dad went back inside to advise the couple what his sweet, innocent little girls had done. He used our shopping money and paid for the eggs, stating we would be back later that day to clean their yard and house.

With shopping no longer on the agenda, we went back home where our parents made us think long and hard about what we had done. All three of us had to get down on our knees and ask God for forgiveness. When we went back to the elderly couple's home, we apologized and began cleaning. Not being the most experienced cleaners, big brother did most of the work. Mom felt Larry bore a lot of the responsibility for not stopping the fiasco. He didn't get the last laugh after all, ha!

When I think about this story, it reminds me of the innocence of children and their willingness to believe anything. Gullible and naïve, it seemed simple and logical to believe Robbie without doubting. Daddy preached about people in the Bible who heard directly from God, surely He could talk to her too! Children have such a pure and uncomplicated form of reasoning. It's understandable why Jesus encourages us to become as a child in our thinking.

> He called a little child and had him stand among them.
> And He said, "I tell you the truth, unless you change and
> become like little children, you will never enter the king-
> dom of heaven. Therefore, whoever humbles himself
> like this child is the greatest in the kingdom of heaven."
> (Matthew 18:2–4 NIV)

Unlike most adults, children believe what you say. If you tell them Santa Claus comes down chimneys and leaves presents at Christmas, they believe you. Even if they do not have a chimney, they still believe. Mom or Dad said it . . . and that settles it. This is how our Heavenly Father longs for us to be toward Him and His Holy Word. If Jesus Christ our Savior said He could and would heal, restore, bless, and prosper us, take Him at His Word. Believe without doubting!

Even if . . . you do not have all the answers.

Even if . . . you do not see how in the world it is possible.

Even if . . . the whole world says you are crazy and fanatical for believing!

We should rejoice just thinking about God's promises instead, we make receiving them so hard. Along the journey, we learn to use so many excuses to justify our lack of faith or unwillingness to walk the path of total submission and obedience. Flesh tells us it is too hard and many times, we feel unworthy. We sit and analyze why the God of heaven and earth should or would ever choose to bless us! Then comes "maturity"; this is where we lose many of the childlike qualities that are so important in our walk with God.

Many years of heartache and pain came and went before I rediscovered the child within longing to get out. I am thankful God is patient and loving toward His children. Little did I realize the safest, happiest, and most fulfilling place to be is in the Master's hands, *falling into a trust relationship* with the *Great I Am!*

Growing up continued to be filled with mischief and miracles; but praise God, no more devil-possessed chickens! Pleasing Daddy became my focus in life. In adoration, I followed him around loving every minute we spent together. He never seemed to mind having a little shadow hanging on his every word.

Each Saturday I accompanied Dad as he visited newcomers to the church and anyone in need of prayer. During one of these weekly visitations another comical event occurred. Our last scheduled stop of the day took us to a woman's house who attended church for the first time the previous Sunday. Wearing only a bikini bathing suit, she laid on a lawn chair sunning in the front yard. In the sixties, the church had many rules and regulations. Mixed swimming and bikinis were just not acceptable, and a respectable woman only wore a whole piece bathing suit, certainly not a two-piece. Seeing a bikini on television was one thing, but seeing one up close shocked and amazed me. To make matters worse, she wore it in front of my daddy!

Instructing me to stay in the car, Dad promised to say a quick hello and leave. Not wanting to miss anything, I rolled down the window and stared intensely as he made his way to this half-naked woman. Greeting her with a handshake Dad handed her a business card, but before he could turn around I loudly hollered out the window, *"Daddy, why are holding that naked woman's hand? I'm telling Mama when we get home!"* Unfortunately, my little eyes did not see him handing her a card, quite the contrary, they saw my daddy holding a half-naked woman's hand! You can imagine the shock and surprise on his poor face as he bolted back to the car.

All the way home, he tried to calm me down. Refusing to listen, I tearfully exclaimed, *"When we get home I'm telling Mommy!"* Pulling into the driveway and before Dad put the car in park; I jumped out and ran inside screaming for Mama. Within minutes, he strolled inside laughing and shaking his head. Unable to see the humor in the situation, I boldly advised Mama of his poor behavior stating he must be punished. She just laughed, gave me a big hug, saying Daddy only held hands with her and his two girls. Unwilling to budge I stood firm, all the while thinking, *"Didn't she hear me? That woman was half-naked. What part of I saw it didn't she understand? I may only be four, but I'm not blind!"* In total frustration, I decided to run away. I grabbed a loaf of bread and a glass of water and headed to my playhouse outside, determined to stay there until they came to their senses!

My parents were totally devoted to one another. Mom always said she never had to worry about Daddy because I kept such a good eye on him, always informing her of any and everything.

Today's society is much more complicated. Children do not often see true devotion, respect, and love, from their parents or caretakers. Many children grow up with only one parent, or not raised by their birth parents at all. There are tragic and sad circumstances all around us. No home is perfect; however, if we will serve and trust God He can do amazing and miraculous things for us, regardless of our situation.

The Lord will perfect that which concerneth me; Thy mercy, oh Lord endureth forever; forsake not the works of Thine own hands.

(Psalm 138:8 KJV)

For the eyes of the Lord range throughout the earth to strengthen those whose hearts are fully committed to Him.

(2 Chronicles 16:9 NIV)

I briefly mentioned the story of Joseph in the first chapter. Let's look a little closer at his life. Talk about a rough childhood! Joseph's brothers were very jealous. They felt their father loved him more than he loved any of them. In fact, the Bible tells us, "... *Israel loved Joseph more than any of his other sons*..." (Genesis 37:3 NIV)

To show Joseph his deep love he made him a beautiful coat of many colors; however, his other sons did not receive one. This only added to their hatred and jealousy. Joseph seemed to make matters worse by telling them about his dream, and how they were all bowing down to him. As their resentment grew, this proved to be more than they could take.

One day when Joseph went to check on his brothers where they were grazing the flock, they threw him in a well and sold him as a slave. This was just the beginning of his nightmare. He would later be falsely accused of rape and thrown into prison.

Through it all, God remained faithful, turning the curses of Joseph's life into blessings. God saw ahead and knew the good plans He had for him, plans the enemy could not destroy. *Joseph suffered much along the way, but claimed victory in the end.*

Put in charge over all of Egypt, he would later be reunited with his family. Read what Joseph said to his brothers many years later.

Then Joseph said to his brothers, "Come close to me.'" When they had done so, he said. "I am your brother Joseph, the one you sold into Egypt! And now, do not be distressed and do not be angry with yourselves for selling me here, because it was to save lives that God sent me ahead of you. For two years now there has been famine in the land, and for the next five years there will not be plowing and reaping. But God sent me ahead of you to preserve for you a rem-

nant on earth and to save your lives by a great deliverance.
So then, it was not you who sent me here, but God. He
made me father to Pharaoh, lord of his entire household
and ruler of all Egypt."

(Genesis 45:4–8 NIV)

The story of Joseph encourages us to trust God with our lives.
Regardless of how dark the circumstance, He truly does have a good
plan for each of us. We may encounter suffering along the way to the
fulfillment of those plans, but it will be worth it all.

I am sure through the years Joseph struggled with many questions. He probably wondered what good could come out of all the
turmoil and injustice he suffered. Would he ever see his father again?
Joseph was sure about one thing, he served a miracle working God.
He feared and loved the Lord. God never forgot about Joseph either.
He faithfully worked all things out, carefully fulfilling the promises
He planned for his life: Restoration of his family, the saving of many
lives, and a life of favor and blessings. Even in suffering, Joseph held
out and never gave up.

It is important to *seek* the Lord for direction, and with patience
wait on Him to answer. We are merely *His* instruments and *His* vessels, used for *His* purposes.

> The Spirit Himself testifies with our spirit that we are
> God's children. Now if we are children, then we are heirs-
> heirs of God and co-heirs with Christ, if indeed we share
> in His sufferings in order that we may also share in His
> glory. I consider that our present sufferings are not worth
> comparing with the glory that will be revealed in us.
>
> (Romans 8:16–18 NIV)

The *Truth* is, like Joseph, we learn obedience through suffering. Jesus
Christ still stands as our greatest example of this very fact.

Although He was a son, *He learned obedience from what He suffered* and, once made perfect, He became the source of eternal salvation for all who obey Him.

(Hebrews 5:8, 9 NIV, emphasis added)

CHAPTER 3

A Childhood Missed

If someone asked what I remembered most about childhood, I would have to say sickness. Although serious health complications did not begin for me until the age of twelve, Mother suffered with a kidney disease and remained sick throughout my childhood. Many nights we were awakened by the sounds of Daddy praying, as he bundled Mom up in preparation to go to the emergency room.

Growing up, we watched mother suffer terrible pain, but through it all, she loved the Lord and possessed an incredible spirit of joy. I am so thankful for a Christian foundation. We made our share of mistakes, but we knew how to pray. This is one of the greatest gifts a parent or caretaker can give to a child.

Dad preached on healing and I believed God could heal Mom. The Bible told story after story of people healed just by asking and believing. I prayed for God to do the same for Mother. Known for being full of questions, I often asked Dad why the Lord allowed her to suffer so much. He always encouraged me to keep praying and one day she would be healed.

Other people had their own opinions as to why Mom continued to be sick. They said things like, *"Maybe it's not God's time or His will to heal your mother."* Even as a child, I knew these opinions did not line up with the scriptures. Although I did not have the answers, Jesus did. One fact remained, the Bible said, *". . . by His stripes we are healed. . ."* and no one could ever convince me Jesus wanted Mom to suffer.

Children have a simple understanding. Without complicating things, they take scripture quite literally. It does not matter how impossible it may seem, their faith is unshakable. A child will pray for something then resume playing, with no worries or lingering doubts. If it says, *"... by His stripes we are healed,"* then we are healed: *End of story!* This was how my mind worked, and I fully expected my prayers to be answered. Once again, we can understand why God desires for us to become as little children, trusting and unpretentious.

The Bible clearly tells us healing is God's will. As you read and study the scriptures, never again will you doubt God's desire for His children to be healthy and abundantly blessed. If someone says, *"it is the Lord's will for you to be sick,"* ask them to show you scripture, which supports their opinion. There simply is not one.

The Bible says, *"Study to show thyself approved unto God, a workman that needeth not to be ashamed, rightly dividing the word of truth"* (2 Timothy 2:15 KJV). We must diligently study and rightly divide the *Word of Truth,* never believing anything that contradicts God's infallible Word!

Jesus died a painful death on the cross conquering death, hell and the grave. His death and resurrection purchased redemption for our sins, and the stripes He bore purchased our healing. If we believe He died for our sins then we must also believe, *"by His stripes we are healed."* The very definition of the word "salvation" includes divine healing, health, prosperity, abundant blessings, and so much more!

We must train ourselves to trust God more than circumstances or the facts as we see them. Believe, even when we do not understand. The key to healing is total unwavering faith and complete trust in God Almighty. Giving into doubt and unbelief hinders God from answering our prayers. The scriptures put it so simply. Why do we choose to complicate them?

As a child, I understood this *truth*. A day would come when my heart could no longer hear the simplicity of God's Word. Complicating it with my own reasoning and human limitations, I found myself searching for the "little girl" who once believed God could do anything. In all my reasoning and searching, the Lord never left my side. He patiently waited for that "little girl" to come out of hiding!

Time went on and Mom continued to battle sickness, yet our hope remained steadfast in God's power to heal. We witnessed the miracle hand of God time after time literally bring her back from death's door, and watched as Dad spent many nights fasting, praying, and pacing the floor. Satan took pleasure in attacking our family with sickness and it was not long before he directed his aim toward me.

My first day of school finally came. Mother had already taught me to read, and I absolutely loved it. She told me there were all kinds of exciting books at school and so many new people to meet. For a "social butterfly" who loved people and books, life could not get any better. Unfortunately, health problems began to show up at the same time I started school.

Petite and finicky, I hated mealtimes, which created stress at home. Food often made me nauseated but finicky really does not begin to describe just how fussy I could be, and soon a series of doctor's visits began. It took many years to discover the blood disease I suffered with, which resulted in a childhood filled with constant health challenges, such as frequent strep throat, bladder and kidney infections, nausea, vomiting, fever, fainting, headaches, and anemia. I often wondered if I'd be sick for the rest of my life, just like Mother. Many nights I climbed in bed with my parents, tearfully pleading with them to pray for God to heal me. Looking back, this must have broken their hearts.

Feeling like a pincushion I hated being sick, and grew tired of the constant shuffle to different doctors hoping to find answers. At bedtime my prayers went something like this: *"Dear Jesus, when I wake up let me be well and never have to go to the doctor again. Thank you Jesus! Amen."*

The enemy wanted to rob me of having a normal childhood by filling my days and nights with sickness and fear. Clearly, he had a stronghold and a generational curse of sickness over our family that desperately needed to be broken.

Satan is continually at war against the Children of God. He uses every opportunity to try to destroy our lives. Sickness and disease seems to be one of his favorite methods of attack. This certainly appeared to be true in our family.

When I look around at all the hospitals, new clinics, medical buildings, and pharmacies, one might think Satan is winning the battle. Be encouraged, this is only temporary. The warrior is rising up in Christians around the world. The enemy's reign of terror will soon end, as Christians yearn for more of God in anticipation of Christ's return. I see a fresh desire growing amongst God's people to seek after *His* heart, to walk in *His* favor, and further the Kingdom of Heaven with the salvation message and the *Truth* of *His* goodness.

Does this mean we will never be sick while on this earth? Unfortunately, no. Don't let this discourage you, *we can be victorious and live an overcoming life!* To accomplish this, we must learn how to overcome with perseverance and a growing faith so that others will want what we have.

Learning the importance of growing my faith did not come easy. Years of spiritual immaturity, ignorance of God's Word, and a lack of understanding cost me dearly. Through it all, God saw my heart and knew I truly loved Him. He extended mercy during those times by gently redirecting my steps, giving me the grace needed to handle the consequences from my choices, and all the while teaching me how to patiently wait and listen for *His* voice.

Whatever we go through in this life it is important to remember we cannot fight Satan using carnal and earthly strategies. Our only hope is in God. We must come against the enemy with the one and only thing that has the power to save, heal, restore, and conquer: The blood of the Lamb and God's precious Holy Word, the *Truth*. To understand what the Bible says, we must read it for ourselves and learn what the promises and benefits are from walking in obedience, then refuse to allow seeds of doubt and unbelief to grow inside our hearts and minds. Thoughts are not the problem; it is how we respond to them. If we will confess our unbelief, cast down negative thoughts and replace them with *Truth*, God will extend forgiveness and mercifully bless our obedience.

When Satan robs and steals from us, the Word of God promises we will get *double* for our trouble! A day of *payback* was in my future and nothing could stop it, including the enemy himself. The past with all its pain and mistakes would be forever covered in the blood of Jesus, never to be used against me again. I did not, nor could I ever, do anything to deserve God's mercy, but faithful and true to His Word, the Lord freely offered it without showing favoritism. What He has done for one, He will do for another.

The Word of God is the same *"yesterday, today, and forever."* A *double* portion, an everlasting covenant filled with joy, love, health, and abundant blessings.

> Instead of their shame my people will receive a *double* portion, and instead of disgrace they will rejoice in their inheritance; and so they will inherit a *double* portion in their land and everlasting joy will be theirs. For I, the Lord, love justice; I hate robbery and iniquity. In my faithfulness I will reward them and make an everlasting covenant with them. Their descendants will be known among the nations and their offspring among the peoples. All who see them will acknowledge that they are a people the Lord has blessed.
> (Isaiah 61:7–9 NIV, emphasis added)

> Return to your fortress, O prisoners of hope; even now I announce that I will restore *twice* as much to you.
> (Zechariah 9:12 NIV, emphasis added)

> After Job had prayed for his friends, the Lord made him prosperous again and gave him *twice* as much as he had before.
> (Job 42:10 NIV, emphasis added)

Serve notice on the enemy today and remind him who your Father is! Do not back down in fear of what terrible attack he may bring. Satan was an angel cast down from heaven due to pride and rebellion. Your Father is his Creator and the Creator of *all* things. Satan cannot create anything. He can only yield a distorted imitation. Father God never has and never will be defeated or surprised by anything Satan devises to bring destruction to our lives. Anything that comes our way must go through the Father, for we belong to Him; therefore, the saying holds true, *"If He brings you to it, He will bring you through it.*" In the name of Jesus and covered by His blood, we will always have the road map to absolute overcoming victory! It is up to us to follow it.

CHAPTER 4

Persistance Pays Off

Healthy and always on the go, I thought Dad was "Superman." We fished, played, and prayed together. Building houses as a side job, he put the extra income he earned into the church. We had a small struggling congregation oppressed by debt, gossip, and backbiting. Feeling God called him to this church, Dad sprang into action working tirelessly to rebuild and restore our wounded congregation. It took a while to get the demons cast out and Saints prayed up, but through obedience and perseverance our little church turned into a loving and growing family.

Arriving home from school one day tragedy struck. Dad suffered a heart attack and had been taken to the hospital. For years, doctors begged him to slow down but he did not listen. Building houses, taking care of our family, and pastoral duties finally took its toll. The added stress of Mom and I being sick did not help matters either. Trying to do everything without any help, Dad failed to heed the warning signs. For a long time God tried to tell him, *"Edward, its okay to ask for help. Lean on Me and I'll carry the burden and lighten the load."*

> Come unto Me, all ye that labor and are heavy laden, and I will give you rest.
>
> (Matthew 11:28 KJV)

Too often, we become so busy *"living"* that we sometimes forget to give our cares and worries to God. We must learn how to rest in Him for He has the answers and wisdom we need. He alone can give us the strength to endure and the ability to bring a harmonic balance in every area of our lives. Many times, we just need to stop and ask for help, but we come up with a hundred reasons why we shouldn't, so we don't!

Mom took us to see Daddy; however, hospital rules stated no one under twelve could go into Intensive Care. Only eleven at the time I thought, *"Surely they won't keep me out,"* but I was wrong.

Relatives from Dad's side of the family continued to pile in as we waited to hear news about his condition. Unfortunately, the Grants have never been known to be quiet or patient! Growing more nervous by the minute, I sat conjuring up ways to get into Dad's room.

The time came for me to make my move and I slowly walked toward the nurse standing guard by the door. I decided to state my case, hoping compassion would over-ride the rules. Taking a deep breath, I went for it. Without hesitation and very curt she said, *"The rules are **not** to be broken!"* Questions filled my mind: *"How can she be so mean? Can't she see my pain? Why is she keeping me from seeing Daddy?"*

Feeling angry and more determined than ever, adrenalin kicked in and something powerful came over me. I hauled off and shoved the nurse aside, burst through the doors, and cried out for Daddy. Hearing the commotion, Mom immediately came out from behind a curtain. She lovingly patted me on the head as I ran to Dad's bedside. Tubes were everywhere but he managed to muster up a reassuring smile. I felt helpless. My mind anxiously raced with thoughts of life without him. I could not help but wonder, *"Who will take care of us?"* Daddy was our rock and we desperately needed him.

Nurse "meanie" soon made her way to Mother, feeling the need to discuss my behavior. I apologized and boldly told her, *"I'll pray for Jesus to teach you how to be nice to hurting people."*

My intentions were never to hurt anyone. Whatever it took, I had to get to Daddy. I could not comprehend why she refused to understand. Apparently, my behavior also disturbed a few of our relatives. Mother told them to leave me alone. Later I found out my parents enjoyed a good chuckle from this little outburst!

Jesus must long for His kids to demonstrate this kind of devotion and determination. If only our love for Him burned so intense we would boldly push aside every hindrance, just to draw close to our Savior. Oh what benefits and blessings await those who strive fearlessly forward and draw near to God.

> Come near to God and He will come near to you...
> (James 4: 8 NIV)

⌒

In Christ alone is fullness of joy. A place of peace and healing; a place of rest for the weary and broken hearted. Even when we fall on our face in failure, in repentance we can give our mess to God. He is the Master of turning a mess into a miracle!

Please understand, we should not aimlessly do whatever we please with the hopes God will bless our mess, but if we are truly repentant and turn from walking the path of disobedience, God is powerful and full of mercy. He will take the curse and bring forth a blessing. My life is proof of this undeniable *truth*.

Once we give our situation over to the Father, usually test and trials follow. During this process, a truly repentant heart will experience a great sense of humility and continue in obedience in spite of the difficulty.

There are times in our walk with Christ our faith *will be tested*. Some of these trials are not a result of disobedience; they are simply part of walking the *"straight and narrow"* and growing in our relationship with Jesus. During these times of testing, we have two choices: *fall* into the pit of despair and unbelief, or *fall* into the hands of God and with perseverance *stand strong*.

A good example of perseverance is the Parable of "The Persistent Widow" in the book of Luke. This widow needed justice against her adversary; however, the judge in the town neither feared God nor cared about men. Jesus spoke this parable to His disciples and asked a very important question.

> Then Jesus told His disciples a parable to show them that they should always pray and not give up. He said, "In a

certain town there was a judge who neither feared God nor cared about men. And there was a widow in that town who kept coming to him with the plea, 'grant me justice against my adversary.' For some time he refused, but finally he said to himself, 'even though I don't fear God or care about men, yet because this widow keeps bothering me, I will see that she gets justice, so that she won't eventually wear me out with her coming!' And the Lord said, 'Listen to what the unjust judge says. And will not God bring about justice for His chosen ones, who cry out to Him day and night? Will He keep putting them off? I tell you, He will see that they get justice, and quickly. However, when the Son of Man comes, will He find faith on the earth?"

(Luke 18:1–8 NIV)

These are the questions we must ask: *"Will He find the kind of faith in me that perseveres in prayer, standing on the Word regardless of the obstacles or circumstances?"* A faith that says, *"I may be in pain but I know my Redeemer lives and purchased my healing on the cross."* A faith that boldly proclaims, *"Though undeserving, I will stand as the Righteousness of Christ and with a grateful heart receive His blessings in my life!"*
God rewards this kind of persistent faith. He is just and merciful. As His children and joint heirs with Christ, we have the assurance of His promises fulfilled.

The Lord mercifully restored Dad back to health. Our church pulled together in love and unity, assisting with household chores, yard work, and wherever there was a need. The family of God can be an awesome thing!
The thought of losing Dad seemed too painful to comprehend. Until he suffered the heart attack, no one realized how heavy his burden had become. Everyone depended on him for one thing or another. It seemed so natural for us to place our confidence in his ability to fix and handle everything. Dad prayed for us when we were

sick, provided for our needs, settled disagreements, and made things right. He truly was our "Superman."

Why did this present such a problem? Our focus and dependence needed to be on Jesus Christ. We were putting too much pressure on Dad to solve all our problems. When dependence is on man, the focus is on works and man's abilities. Man is limited God is not. Once this happens, our priorities get out of line according to God's Word. No longer allowing ourselves to grow and mature, we end up placing too much of a burden on someone else to come to our rescue.

There are times when seeking counsel is necessary and full of wisdom; however, as Children of God we carry a responsibility. Instead of running elsewhere for answers about every little thing, we need to walk close enough to the Father and boldly approach the "*Throne of Grace*" for ourselves: As His children, we have this right!

Too often, we hear about churches splitting and people turning away from God because of something a pastor, prophet, or teacher has done. Our foundation must be built on the Rock, Jesus Christ. Nothing or no one should be able to shake us off that foundation. How shameful it is for us to allow the mistakes of mere man to interfere or hurt our relationship with a Loving and Faithful Father!

Challenges and obstacles should be communicated in prayer to our Creator, our Deliverer. To successfully grow and mature we must *pray, listen,* and *apply* as we *rise up* and *exercise our faith.*

I grew up running to Dad for everything, especially spiritual matters. This is okay if you are a child, but as you spiritually mature, your first instinct should be to seek Christ. My first thought usually went like this, *"Dad will have the answer. I don't really need to pray, I'll just ask him."*

This pattern of misplaced priorities repeated itself throughout my life, until one day I asked God for wisdom. He quickly shined a spotlight on this immature area and the Holy Spirit began a new work of maturity and growth. I am sure Dad breathed a sigh of relief when this *growing up phase* started manifesting itself in my actions. Although he never complained, I am certain my problems felt overwhelming to him at times.

Life soon resumed to what we called "normal." Mom and I continued to battle sickness as uncertain obstacles lay ahead. Even in our weaknesses and human frailties, God remained faithful. He is Jehovah-Shammah, the God who promises to never leave or forsake us.

> The Lord Himself goes before you and will be with you; He will never leave you nor forsake you. Do not be afraid, do not be discouraged.
>
> (Deuteronomy 31:8 NIV)

> Then thou shalt call, and the Lord shall answer; thou shalt cry, and He shall say, Here I am...
>
> (Isaiah 58:9 KJV)

> But I am poor and needy; yet the Lord thinketh upon me; Thou art my help and my deliverer; make no tarrying, O my God."
>
> (Psalm 40:17 KJV)

CHAPTER 5

The Difference Between Hope and Faith

While studying Luke chapter twenty-four, I began to understand the difference between hope and faith. After the crucifixion, two followers of Jesus were traveling the road to Emmaus discussing everything that had happened. As they traveled along, Jesus Himself came up and began walking with them, (but they were divinely kept from recognizing Him). He asked what they were discussing, and they were amazed this man did not know what happened in Jerusalem. With great sadness, they proceeded to explain the situation.

> He was a prophet, powerful in word and deed before God and all the people. The chief priests and our rulers handed Him over to be sentenced to death, and they crucified Him; *but we had hoped He was the One who was going to redeem Israel.*
> (Luke 24: 19–21 NIV, emphasis added)

These men *"had hoped"* Jesus was the One to set Israel free, which is why they were so disappointed in the recent events of His death; however, prior to the crucifixion Jesus told them in Luke 9:22 that He would be raised to life on the third day. *Where was their faith?* When their own women could not find His body and said they saw a vision of angels stating He was alive, *where was their faith?* After all, it was the third day! When some of their companions went to the tomb and found what the women said to be true, *where was their faith?* They *"had hope,"* so *where was their faith* and why didn't they believe? In fact, in Luke 24:25 Jesus called them *"foolish and slow of heart to believe."*

When He was at the table with them, He took bread, gave thanks, broke it and began to give it to them. Then their eyes were opened and they recognized Him, and He disappeared from their sight. They asked each other, 'Were not our hearts burning within us while He talked with us on the road and opened the Scriptures to us?

(Luke 24:30–32 NIV)

We all need hope but when hope is mixed with faith, we have a *powerful combination!* These men *hoped* in the Savior but they lacked *faith.* After His death, they were even reluctant to call Him the Messiah.

Psalm 62:5 tells us to, *"Find rest, O my soul, in God alone; my hope comes from Him."* Our hope is in God, but it is our faith that makes the decision to believe in Him and boldly, *". . . call things that are not as though they were!"* (Romans 4:17 NIV, emphasis added)

Every personality test I have ever taken always reveals the same thing; I am an extrovert and optimistic by nature. I have been told these are good traits to have, however, at some point in my spiritual growth I needed to allow this "hopeful optimism" to mix with a "growing faith." Instead, I stayed in an *"I'm hoping for the best, and I hope God will heal me"* frame of mind. This mind-set created a perfect atmosphere for *defeat* and *hopelessness.* The next stage of my life shined a spotlight on how desperately I needed to understand not only the difference, but how to combine *hope* and *faith.*

The remainder of my childhood and throughout adolescence, I continued to experience frequent fainting spells, severe bladder and kidney infections, migraine headaches, female problems, and anemia. My white cell count stayed extremely high due to infections, which resulted in hospitalizations to undergo a series of antibiotic treatments.

Examined and treated by numerous physicians, they could not figure out what was wrong with my blood. Characteristics of the illness appeared much like leukemia and other diseases, but test after test came back negative for everything they suspected.

The doctors did agree on one diagnosis, a small bladder tube (urethra). For the next several years, every thirty to sixty days, I went through a painful dilation procedure in an effort to minimize infections and open up the urethra.

The Bible says, *"The joy of the Lord is our strength."* Being the ultimate optimist, early in life I purposed in my heart to be known as "the happy one," not "the sick one." Although this attitude of joy did not please the enemy, I stayed determined. When laughter and joy seemed far away, I took comfort in the scriptures.

> A merry heart doeth good like a medicine, but a broken spirit drieth the bones.
>
> (Psalm 17:22 KJV)

> ...for I have learned to be content whatever the circumstances. I know what it is to be in need and I know what it is to have plenty. I have learned the secret of being content in any and every situation, whether well fed or hungry, whether living in plenty or in want, I can do all things through Him who gives me strength.
>
> (Philippians 4:11–13 NIV)

Shortly after turning fifteen, my urologist requested permission to perform an experimental surgery, in an attempt to correct the urethra. Children were good candidates for the procedure but due to my age, they barely gave a 10% chance of success. Regardless, infections were spreading my kidneys and growing more frequent and painful. Grasping for help, we said yes.

During surgery, our family and friends gathered together and prayed. We fully believed God heard our prayers and the surgery would bring healing for my bladder condition. Unfortunately, I was not prepared for what happened next. Within a few weeks, the doctors realized the procedure had failed. Confused and depressed, nothing made sense anymore.

Disappointed and apologetic, doctors tried to encourage us by stating the field of medicine changed at a phenomenal pace, and a breakthrough could be just around the corner for patients with my problem. Having grown tired of reassuring word, I turned away and secretly thought, *"Can't they fix at least one thing that is wrong with me!"*

Have you ever prayed and believed God so hard for something but you did not get the answer you expected? During those times it is hard to be strong, and unfortunately, the enemy knows this. When we are weak and confused, he takes every opportunity to devise a *pity poor me* trap. At this point, I readily obliged him and joy no longer prevailed in my world of self-pity and unanswered questions.

I began asking, *"Lord, where are You, and why didn't You answer my prayer?"* I do not believe God gets upset when we ask questions; however, my heart had become accusatory and bitter. This self-destructive attitude allowed the enemy to steal away my peace and joy, replacing it with fear and discouragement.

You may be at a place of desperation in your own life, a place where nothing makes sense. You have done all you know to do, and it still is not enough. You may even be questioning God as you seek answers to difficult questions. Have you ever felt like screaming, *"God, where are You, do You hear me? Do You care? Do You love me?"*

Due to the fall of man, Satan is the ruler of this world and we are his prey. Scripture tells us, *". . . and whoever shuns evil becomes prey"* (Isaiah 59:15 NIV). Because of this, God is always at work on our behalf and warring against the enemy's attacks, but there are times we may never fully understand a situation or have an answer. It is in those moments of frustration we need a maturing, growing faith. In moments of despair and uncertainty, it is vital we learn to *"lean not on our own understanding . . ."* (Proverbs 3:5) and trust the Lord Almighty to *"make our paths straight"* (Proverbs 3:6).

Be encouraged and remember an important *Truth*—God is more powerful than Satan is, and He gave us a promise, *"A righteous man may have many troubles, but the Lord delivers him from them all"* (Psalm 34:19 NIV).

God's Word does not say we will understand all our troubles, but it does say He will *"deliver us from them all."* Although we are not promised a life of ease free from worry and problems, we are promised deliverance; this *Truth* brings a great deal of peace to my soul!

Have you ever watched a cat stalk its prey? Slowly and methodically it moves, with its eyes fixed on the target. Nothing can distract it. Satan preys on the Children of God in this same way. The only way of escape is to *know, trust in,* and *apply God's Word.* We must fix our eyes and ears on our Creator, no other report should be trusted. Even when things do not make sense, our *complete hope and faith* must be in the resurrection power of Jesus Christ! The slightest distraction due to unbelief, anxiety, or pain, gives Satan the opportunity to *"kill, steal, and destroy."*

> Be sober, be vigilant, because your adversary the devil, as a roaring lion, walketh about seeking whom he may devour.
> (1 Peter 5:8 NIV)

As you continue reading my life's story, you will understand why I emphasize *knowing the Word* and *trusting God.* Too many times I crashed and burned due to believing Satan's lies. My eyes failed to *stay fixed on Jesus* and *His report.* A "need to analyze and understand" became a source of great downfall.

Humans look at things through the eyes of flesh. If we could see our circumstances through spiritual eyes, doubt and fear would not overwhelm us. You see, God is not going to allow anything to come into our lives *for which He is not willing and able to bring us through!*

There is a great story in the Bible regarding seeing with spiritual eyes. The King of Aram was at war with Israel. The prophet Elisha, warned the King of Israel where the Arameans would be. The Israelites were repeatedly one step ahead of them. This enraged the King of Aram, so he summoned his officers together to find out who the traitor was among them.

"None of us, my lord the king," said one of his officers, "but Elisha, the prophet who is in Israel, tells the king of Israel the very words you speak in your bedroom." "Go, find out where he is, the king ordered, so I can send men and capture him." The report came back: "He is in Dothan." Then he sent horses and chariots and a strong force there. They went by night and surrounded the city. When the servant of the man of God got up and went out early the next morning, an army with horses and chariots had surrounded the city. "Oh my lord, what shall we do?" the servant asked. *"Don't be afraid"* the prophet answered, *"Those who are with us are more than those who are with them."* And Elisha prayed, *"O Lord open his eyes so he may see."* *Then the Lord opened the servant's eyes, and he looked and saw the hills full of horses and chariots of fire all around Elisha.*

(2 Kings 6:12–17 NIV, emphasis added)

In response to Elisha's prayer, his servant was able to see the protecting, mighty, and heavenly host surrounding them. What an amazing boost of faith!

The devil wants our spiritual eyes blinded with lies and deceptions. Keeping our focus on flesh and circumstances always gives him the upper hand. We have to build up the *spirit man* by feeding on the Word of God and speaking *Truth* over our situation.

Walk in daily communion with the Holy Spirit; purpose to take in more of God and His Word than the world and its lies. Begin to watch and weigh every word before speaking. Miracles manifest when we do these things. Remember, we are prey to Satan; therefore, we must put on the armor of God to fight against his attacks!

Do not be afraid to reveal everything to the Father in prayer. You see, He already knows. Nothing you can say will ever make Him stop loving you. He longs for us to commune with Him. Don't just talk to God when you're hurting or in need. Talk to Him when you are happy and full of joy. He loves an honest and grateful heart full of praise.

How would our earthly parents feel if we only talked to them when we needed or wanted something? This kind of selfish and self-centered attitude will cause any relationship to suffer. Too often, this is how we treat God.

We have a direct line to this magnificent "Creator of Life" through prayer, communion, praise, and obedience. *Reading God's Word and talking to Him daily should come as naturally as eating and breathing. Having the Truth of the Living God inside us and acting on it will turn Satan's attacks into awesome opportunities for the Lord to reveal Himself as our Healer, Deliverer, the Great I Am!*

I grew up talking to the Lord, but rarely listening. I failed to realize a healthy mature relationship consists of *two* people communicating. We limit His ability to bless and manifest miracles in our lives when we are doing all the talking. You see, He is the one with the answers. I am so thankful He remained patiently at work in my heart.

You may ask, *"How does God talk to someone?"* He speaks in many ways. I have found the majority of the time He speaks to me through His Word and the Holy Spirit, *"that still small voice."* What is *"that still small voice"*? Scriptures explain, once we receive Christ, that the Holy Spirit dwells within us. It is a *Living Spirit of God* constantly directing and instructing us to walk according to His Word.

Several times in my life, God has spoken to me in an audible voice. This is truly a humbling experience. He can also speak through dreams, visions, prophets, and ministers. *Do not box God in; He can speak any way He chooses.* The Bible tells us in the book of Numbers, chapter twenty-two, that He even spoke through a donkey!

I feel it is necessary to issue a caution, we must not carelessly and loosely state, *"God spoke to me and said . . ."* unless He truly did. It is a violation of the commandment, *"Thou shall not take the name of the Lord thy God in vain."* The amplified version of this verse brings a sobering clarity to this commandment.

You shall not use or repeat the name of the Lord your God in vain (that is, lightly frivolously, in false affirma-

tion or profanely); for the Lord will not hold him guilt-
less who takes His name in vain.

(Exodus 20:7 TAB)

Yes, God speaks to His children but too often, He gets credit for
things He had nothing to do with! There are hurting people who are
in desperate situations and just because someone told them, *"God
spoke to me and said (so and so) and you should do (such and such)"* they
have ended up with additional pain and devastation. This one statement has caused so much damage within the Body of Christ.

If someone constantly says, *"God spoke"* a big red flag goes up
and I begin observing the fruit and life of that individual. This is not
judging, it is doing what scripture tells us to do, *"test everything"* (we
will discuss this scripture further in a later chapter). I have heard
people say God said *"so and so"* and when it does not work out, they
claim He changed His mind. In 1 Samuel 15:29 it clearly says, *"For
He is not a man, that He should change His mind."* Malachi 3: 6 states,
"I the Lord do not change."

You may argue that God changed His mind several times in the
Old Testament. However, as you study the Bible, you will discover it
had to do with a repentant heart that turned from sin and got back
on track. This is why intercession for the lost and those who stray
from the Lord is of critical importance. God will always reserve the
right to bring redemption instead of wrath when repentance has
been chosen over sin (Ezekiel 33:13–20). God does not call someone
to do a certain thing to only recant and say, *"Oops, sorry, I changed My
mind!"* Study this for yourself and it will help you discern the *Truth.*

When I feel God has spoken to me about something that has to
do with another individual, *first* I make sure what I heard lines up
with God's Word. *Next,* I ask the Lord to show me if this is something I am to intercede and pray about, or share with that person.
If it is something I am to share, I begin the conversation by saying,
"Take this to God in prayer and ask Him to confirm the truth."

I do not want to assume at any time I am not capable of making
a mistake. I am an emotional woman who is sensitive and hormonal!
If I am in error (and yes, it has happened), I am the first to say, *"for-*

give me." When it is God, the Holy Spirit will reveal the *truth* and *confirm* what has been said. The fact is, we are fallible; humans make mistakes but God does not. One more thing to remember, the fruit will follow. *Inspect the fruit and the truth will be clear!*

Throughout my life, different individuals have given me *words from God;* usually my spirit will immediately bear witness or I will feel strangely uneasy. Regardless, I carefully weigh the words against the Bible. If it checks out, I give it to the Lord and ask for confirmation (unless He has already confirmed it).

> Jesus answered, "I did tell you, but you do not believe. The miracles I do in My Father's name speak for Me, but you do not believe because you are not My sheep. My sheep listen to My voice; I know them, and they follow Me. I give them eternal life, and they shall never perish; no one can snatch them out of My hand. My Father who has given them to Me is greater than all, no one can snatch them out of My Father's hand. I and the Father are one."
>
> (John 10:25–30 NIV)

What a glorious promise! *We can hear the voice of God and no one can snatch us out of His mighty hands.* We are His sheep, He is our Shepherd. Talk to your Shepherd, ask Him to open your spiritual eyes and ears; you will find He is just waiting to reveal Himself to you in wonderful and exciting ways!

CHAPTER 6

Little Miss Worry Wart

I eventually stopped pouting about the failed surgery and asking, *"Why, why, why?"* It amazes me that God never screamed, *"Shut-up Donna, you are driving me crazy!"* Thank goodness, He is not impatient like so many of us (myself included). I am just thankful He lovingly and patiently stuck around.

Another year would pass filled with many challenges, but faithful and true to His Word, the Lord stayed by my side, always wooing me to draw closer. One Sunday morning a few weeks before my sixteenth birthday, a young man walked into our church. Sitting at the piano preparing the music, I looked up and watched him as he made his way to a seat. Stepping down from the platform, I went over to welcome him to the service. He introduced himself as Bob Wilcox, stating he was in the Air Force and stationed at Eglin. Bob appeared quiet and shy and although I could not put my finger on it, there was something about the guy I really liked. We were immediately drawn to one another and a close friendship soon developed.

Bob possessed a presence of someone who trusted God with his life. You did not have to ask, you just knew he loved the Lord. We enjoyed spending time together and he always made me feel accepted and happy. Being the typical teenager, I did not know how to appreciate this gift of friendship, nor did I recognize God's hand at work.

In time, our friendship blossomed into courtship, but feeling like a burden due to sickness and scared of getting to close, I withdrew and became distant. In my heart, I felt he deserved better than I could ever give him. Bob put up with a lot during our on-again off-again relationship.

Instead of seeking God for guidance, I reasoned things out for myself. Unfortunately, a teenager does not possess much wisdom. During those young and impressionable years, I became a slave to feelings. Someone once said, *"Feelings make great servants but terrible masters."* This is a very wise statement!

In spite of spiritual immaturity, when I fell on my face in failure I earnestly sought God for help and answers. The desire to serve Him remained strong. Even when I chose the wrong path, God used those very mistakes to teach and mold me into something useful for His glory.

Sunday nights after church our youth group often went out for pizza or burgers. We shared many hours of laughter and mischievous fun. The Bible tells us a cheerful heart is medicine to the body, and it certainly lifted my spirits. Very few people understood the importance I placed on these little outings. For a short while I forgot about pain and sickness, as it brought a sense of normalcy and much-needed laughter. Christian friends and fellowship are necessary and vitally important in our walk with God.

Physically things took a turn for the worse. Serious female complications surfaced with unpredictable and heavy menstrual periods, followed by ovarian cysts. As doctors continued running test, constant anemia, fainting spells, and numerous infections sent me in and out of the emergency room and hospital for treatment. Everyone remained baffled, unable to find the reason why my white cell count stayed so high and infections plagued me continuously.

There were other problems as well. Always the perfectionist, I desired to please everyone. With high expectations and overly critical of myself, anxieties often turned to constant worry. This behavior eventually caused a bleeding ulcer, resulting in more hospitalizations and additional daily medications.

One semester in High School, I received a B in Home Economics on my report card, sending my world crashing down around me because a B ruined my A average. Feeling as though I let everyone down, I cried all the way home on the school bus. Mother tried to console me, but nothing worked. Finally, she called the teacher requesting a conference. The teacher was sympathetic and advised

Mother I could do a make up assignment. In those days Home Economics consisted of sewing and cooking. I cooked without a problem, but sewing frustrated me something awful. Fortunately, Mom sewed beautifully and gave me the instructions needed to bring my grade up to an A. I still remember her reassuring voice saying, *"Okay little Miss Worry Wart, it's not the end of the world!"*

In and out of the hospital so frequently, I could no longer continue attending high school. The principle and teachers were kind and helpful towards my entire family. They helped Mother make the necessary arrangements for me to complete my studies at home and receive my diploma.

The year I turned eighteen, my parents surprised me with a very special gift by arranging for me to record a gospel album. Singing and testifying about Jesus is all I ever wanted to do and suddenly the dream seemed to be materializing. As the day approached I nervously prayed, *"Dear Lord, please don't allow health complications to land me in the hospital and hinder the album."*

God heard my prayer and granted me the strength to complete the project. Whatever the cost I purposed to work for Him until I died, but the devil did not like this stubborn determination and he did not plan to sit idly by.

> Humble yourselves, therefore, under God's mighty hand, that He may lift you up in due time. Cast all your anxiety on Him because He cares for you. Be self-controlled and alert. Your enemy the devil prowls around like a roaring lion looking for someone to devour.
>
> (1 Peter 5:6–8 NIV)

Word about the album spread as churches began asking me to come for concerts and services. Health complications made it apparent I could not travel alone. My cousin Rhonda and I were very close and she lived only a short distance away in Pensacola, Florida. She had been earnestly seeking God's will for a new direction in her life. Although Rhonda shared my desire to reach the lost, the thought of public speaking made her panic and break out in a sweat. Despite being extremely shy and quiet, the Lord put it on her heart to become my traveling companion. It is amazing how God knows just who and what to bring into our lives to fulfill His will and purposes!

Rhonda lovingly and meticulously handled details like driving and equipment set up. She also possessed the precious gift of prayer and intercession. Our opposite natures worked well together as her mature, mild manner brought a balance to my hyperactive personality.

Being in ministry with me held many challenges such as I fainted easily and with no warning whatsoever. One minute we were driving down the road or walking through a grocery store talking and laughing, and then *bam*, I would pass out cold! We always seemed to find humor in the situation. At the time, it sure beat crying.

I suffered with intense migraines, severe pain in my back and sides, infections, and high temperatures. Traveling to and from services often found us pulled over on the side of a highway, with me throwing up. It was not a pretty sight! Through it all, Rhonda's prayers carried us from destination to destination with the patience and compassion of a saint. Amazingly, it is the laughter and times of prayer I remember most, not the pain or frustration.

Together we witnessed God move on our behalf in mighty and miraculous ways. Pulling up to a church or service, we prayed for God's healing touch and anointing. The Lord never let us down, as soon as I stepped on the platform or stage all nausea and pain immediately disappeared. Singing my heart out, I testified and prayed for people. In those moments, I felt a faith strong enough to move any mountain. When service ended and we headed home, sickness usually returned with a vengeance.

One night in a small country church, a lady came forward for prayer. She desired healing from a kidney infection. Standing there with a kidney infection myself, I thought, *"How in the world can I pray for this lady and expect results?"* Suddenly, a warrior-type spirit arose within me and I began speaking God's Word of healing over her body. The Lord miraculously healed her and the fever and pain immediately disappeared! I spent years confused, wandering why God did not heal me too. The truth is, I could believe for her but not for myself. The answer was quite simple, I needed to grow my faith and believe I was just as worthy of healing as that dear sweet lady!

I studied the Word of God and thought I knew what it said; however, I lacked understanding on how to apply it. I could not see myself through God's eyes. Instead, I saw an *"always going to be sick, this is my cross to bear"* image staring back at me.

"Accepting and tolerating" limited God's ability to perform a greater miracle in my life. The devil deceived me into thinking I somehow deserved this, therefore it must be God's will. In the South, we call this *stinkin' thinkin,'* and it will **always** hinder **God's best** in our lives! Whether we realize it or not, when we choose to entertain these kinds of thoughts, we are believing lies and are no longer in agreement with God. Christ died and shed His precious blood so that everyone could be saved, healed, blessed, and walk in divine health. We are meant to be *overcomers.*

Jesus desired for me to be an overcomer all the time, not just when I ministered. Without openly admitting it, I suffered with a works mentality. I thought if I worked hard enough for God, eventually He'd consider me worthy for healing. It is not about works, talents, abilities, or how many scriptures we can quote! The Bible clearly states, *"our righteousness is as filthy rags."* Working for God nonstop will not make us good enough. The *Truth* is, just like salvation healing is a gift, free to all *by faith* and purchased on Calvary *by the blood of Jesus Christ.*

During this time, God performed a miracle in our family. One afternoon, a young military man from our church who loved Mom dearly came over to pray for her. He knew her kidneys were damaged and without divine intervention, her condition would deteriorate. As they prayed, Mother felt something powerful and warm go through her entire body. From that day forward Mom's kidneys functioned properly. She was healed! This gave fresh hope to our family and needed encouragement for the days ahead.

My life continued to be interrupted with doctors and hospitals. Forced to face the inevitable, I could no longer travel. Rhonda and I said goodbye to our days on the road but never stopped believing for a miracle. In spite of the setbacks, the Lord found ways to use us for His glory.

God is not looking for perfect vessels to get the job done. Only His Son can fill those shoes. All He truly wants is a heart and life striving after Him in willing obedience.

CHAPTER 7

Please God Take Me Home

During one of my bouts with sickness, a cyst developed on my left ovary with a serious infection. Before long, my bladder and both kidneys were also infected, sending my white cell count soaring dangerously high. Running out of options, doctors scheduled a partial hysterectomy and exploratory surgery. I panicked when I heard the word *hysterectomy*, but they assured me I could still have children one day, and with any luck, the exploratory surgery might reveal some answers. We did not believe in luck but we believed in prayer, and that is what we did . . . *Pray!*

They did not find the answers they hoped for, but I did receive some pain relief for a brief period; however, this only proved to be a small lull before a very troubling storm.

With traveling behind me and after a time of recuperating, I resumed working with the music and youth department in Dad's church. This was not a paid position, so I went in search of a job. When you live in a small town, everyone knows you or knows of you and because of my numerous health problems, I wasn't sure anyone would be willing to hire me. God's favor shined through and He mercifully opened a door of opportunity at a local bank with great health benefits. Because of my physical condition, I could not get insurance on my own and this proved to be a huge blessing.

The next few months, life played out like a nightmare. I was extremely thin, and everyday presented discouragement and physical pain. Regardless of how hard I tried, I could not seem to catch a break. Due to heavy medications, I suffered with memory loss, a poor appetite, and confusion. My employer never knew what physical disaster might strike from one week to the next. Through it all, God's mercy and favor prevailed.

One night after coming home from work, I passed out several times. I was experiencing severe pain in my sides, excessive menstrual bleeding, and a high temperature. My parents frantically called the doctor and they rushed me to the emergency room. In my heart, I knew something bad was happening. With the hospital forty-five minutes away and not knowing what lay ahead, I saw the desperation in Mom and Dad's eyes. We all prayed together as fear gripped our hearts.

What a scary time this must have been for them, and as the years passed we rarely spoke about that long ride to the hospital. Parents want to fix things for their kids, but they could not fix this or simply kiss and make it go away.

The enemy comes in like a flood when we are weak from praying, vulnerable from sleepless nights, and tired from pain and worry. He attacks without mercy when we are physically and emotionally weary from praying for a miracle we are not seeing. It is in those moments the Word of God must be rooted deep in our hearts. Beyond a shadow of doubt, beyond all circumstances, and no matter how hard or painful we must know *God is willing and able to keep His Word!* If we do not stay focused on *Truth*, Satan's attacks will beat us down.

I do not mind telling you, we were worn out from the struggle and things were going downhill fast. Everyone prayed for a miracle while a team of doctors hovered about discussing their next plan of attack. Feeling they must have overlooked something from the previous surgery, they decided to go back in. In no shape to argue or question, they assured me everything possible would be done to avoid a complete hysterectomy. I was terrified!

Weary from pain and uncertainty, I prayed for God to heal me or take me home. Before heading off to surgery I reminded my parents, *"If things look really bad God will give us a miracle, don't worry and have faith. I don't want a hysterectomy."*

Family members began arriving. Amanda, my three-year-old niece, is who I remember most from that night. She was a sweet bundle of joy and best of all she loved her Aunt Donna. Judy, Amanda's mom, hid her in a laundry basket to sneak her into the room. She crawled up in bed next to me patting my face, telling me Jesus was going to make it all better. She appeared so full of faith while the rest of us felt overwhelmed by the circumstances and bad reports.

Amanda's childlike faith is what God longs for us to demonstrate toward His Word even in the worst of times. When life throws us a curve and does not seem fair, childlike faith is often hard to find. That's when we have to *dig deep* and *choose Truth*!

Small and frail, doctors worked to stabilize and prepare me for surgery. Little did I know in a few short hours my faith would experience a tremendous blow, and life would be forever changed.

During surgery, I began losing a lot of blood and my pressure dropped dangerously low. My female organs were in terrible shape and I continued to hemorrhage. The situation turned critical quickly and it appeared the doctor's efforts were failing. In a desperate attempt to turn the situation around, one of the physicians went to the surgical waiting room and asked for permission to proceed with a hysterectomy. With pressure mounting, my parents said yes. I received numerous pints of blood that day, which put me at risk for other complications. In 1979, blood was not being tested for the AIDS virus. Years later, God's mercy and protection from this fatal disease revealed itself in a miraculous way!

Waking up in recovery I asked for Mom and Dad. Hardly able to talk due to tubes and needles everywhere, I whispered, *"Everything's okay isn't it? They didn't have to do the hysterectomy did they?"* Tears rolled down Daddy's face and he said, *"Baby, you are going to be okay, they got everything."* Asking him what he meant, he said the doctors did not have a choice, the hysterectomy was necessary. Seeing my pain and despair, Mama said, *"Donna, don't worry about not being able to have children, you've had enough pain in your life and God has great things in store for you."* Something happened to me in that moment. I can't explain it except to say I felt as though a part of me died that day. Living lost its appeal. Feeling hopeless I prayed a simple prayer, *"Please God, take me home. I don't want to live here anymore."*

The crushing disappointment of only being nineteen-years-old and robbed of ever having children along with continued constant pain hindered my ability to remember, *"When bad things happen, God is still on the throne."* I went through a season of anger and bitterness toward God for allowing the hysterectomy. I even felt He added insult to injury by choosing to let me live, especially with what happened next.

As for my parents, I never felt anger toward them because of the hysterectomy. I realized they were desperately trying to save my life the only way they knew how. Ultimately, God had the final say. Even in this season of rebellion, His love and protection stayed faithful. He is an amazing Father and His love is unconditional.

Nothing takes God by surprise! He knew what would happen that fateful day. Did this stop His plans for me, *Oh No!* His plans were going to be wonderfully accomplished in spite of the enemies' attempts to *kill and destroy.* The road ahead stretched long and hard, but blessings would come from the curse!

To this day, I truly believe if the hysterectomy had not happened God would have miraculously sustained my life, for He is the *"Giver and Taker of Life."* I would not have left this world until He fulfilled and accomplished everything He planned. His Word promises, *"The Lord will fulfill His purpose for me"* (Psalm 138:8 NIV); *"Being confident in this, that He who began a good work in you will carry it on to completion until the day of Christ Jesus"* (Philippians 1:6 NIV).

You may ask, *"Well Donna, what if you died on the operating table?"* The answer is simple; I am still alive today so obviously God's work in my life was not finished. I am His child and I belong to Him alone. I will not die until the Father says its time.

> Blessed is he who has regard for the weak; the Lord delivers him in times of trouble. The Lord will protect him and preserve his life; He will bless him in the land and not surrender him to the desire of his foes. The Lord will sustain him on his sickbed and restore him from his bed of illness.
>
> (Psalms 41:1–3 NIV)

The greatest weapon we can use in moments of pain and confusion is *praise*. Years would pass before I understood the power of this "praise principle." The Bible says, *"Be joyful always; pray continually; give thanks in all circumstances, for this is God's will for you in Christ Jesus"*(1 Thessalonians 5:16, 17, 18 NIV).

Trusting God is a 100% commitment, even when He does not make sense and seems a million miles away. We must trust Him when the outcome is totally different than we think it should be; when there have been no revelations and no *"still small voice."* We must remain steady and willing to stand firm with unwavering faith even though we cannot see or understand a *reason for* or *reason why* we are facing certain situations and challenges. God rewards this kind of faith and it is essential in fighting spiritual warfare and receiving a miracle.

Shadrach, Meshach, and Abednego were three young men who understood this principle and knew what it meant to trust God. King Nebuchadnezzar was furious because they would not bow down to his image of gold. With conviction, they stood firm…even if it meant death.

> If we are thrown into the blazing furnace, *the God we serve is able to save us* from it, and *He will rescue us from your hand, O King. But even if He does not,* we want you to know O King, that we will not serve your god or worship the image of god you have set up.
>
> (Daniel 3:17, 18 NIV, emphasis added)

Wow, I love how boldly they spoke. Their decision to trust God regardless of the outcome is an amazing testimony of passion and courage. Even if He did not deliver them, these young men purposed to stay true and faithful. Did God let them down? Absolutely Not! He rewarded their faith and delivered them in a miraculous way.

When I meditate on this story it leaves me with a question, *"Will He find this kind of faith in me?"* You may want to take inventory and ask yourself that same question.

CHAPTER 8

Honeysuckle and Vanilla

When doctors came in with their facts our faith took a beating, but God's mercy continued to carry us through. You see, God is not interested in the facts. Gathering and receiving information about any situation is using wisdom, but it does not determine the outcome. Facts and information enables us to be specific and focused in prayer, however, the only true and unmovable report is *God's Truth.* We must ask, *"What does He say about our lives? Does His Word say we are to be sick or well, poor or blessed?"*

In Numbers chapter fourteen, Moses sent spies to explore the land of Canaan. They returned reporting the facts as they saw them with their natural eyes. In summary they said, *"Are you crazy? We cannot attack those people; they are too big and strong. We seemed like grasshoppers next to them. We would have been better off if we died in Egypt or in the desert."*

Their report angered God. He called it an evil or bad report. Why? Did they lie? No. So what was the problem? Let's look at the scriptures in both the New International and King James Versions.

> They gave Moses this account: "We went into the land to which you sent us, and it does flow with milk and honey! Here is its fruit. But the people who live there are powerful and the cities are fortified and very large. We even saw descendants of Anak there…"
>
> (Numbers 13:27, 28 NIV)

Then Caleb silenced the people before Moses and said; "We should go up and take possession of the land, *for we can certainly do it.*" But the men who had gone up with him said we can't attack those people; they are stronger than we are. And they spread among the Israelites a bad report. *They said, "The Land we explored devours those living in it. All the people we saw there are of great size. We saw the Nephilim there (the descendants of Anak come from the Nephilim). We seemed like grasshoppers in our own eyes, and we looked the same to them."*
(Numbers 13:30–33 NIV, emphasis added)

And they brought up an evil report *of the land...*
(Numbers 13:32 KJV, emphasis added)

Rather than trust the God who brought them this far, the Israelites chose to believe the unbelieving fact finders and continued to grumble. Well, guess what! Those fact-finding reporters were struck down with a plague and died, while the generation they influenced would live out there lives in the desert, never to see the "Promised Land."

Only Joshua and Caleb came back telling everyone the same God that parted the Red Sea, performed miraculous signs and wonders in Egypt and the desert, supplied food, water, and prevented their clothes from wearing out, would go before them making a way. Joshua and Caleb were blessed for their trust in God and allowed to enter the land.

Why is faith in God so important? The Word says without it we cannot please our Father. One interpretation of *"please"* in Greek is, *"to come into full agreement."* When we choose to believe and speak things that are contrary to the *Truth*, (God's Word) we are choosing to come out of agreement with God ... Our Creator ... Our Father! In doing this we are actually saying, *"God, I really don't trust You."*

Too often, we allow our trust in God to be hindered because He did not meet our needs. God answers prayer according to faith, not need. If God answered according to need, there would be no purpose or reason for faith! We all fall short in this area at one time or another, but we must learn the *Truth* and grow.

When we quit *hearing* the Word of God, we don't receive. Faith comes by *hearing* the Word. Once we *hear*, then we can choose to do something important, *obey*. What does obedience look like? Someone willing to *believe, receive, and expect!*

After the hysterectomy, I felt God let me down because He did not meet my needs. Like the spies sent to explore the land of Canaan, focusing only on the facts opened doors of doubt and unbelief in my heart.

> Therefore, we do not lose heart, though outwardly we are wasting away, yet inwardly, we are being renewed day by day. For our light and momentary troubles are achieving for us eternal glory that far outweighs them all. *So we fix our eyes not on what is seen, but on what is unseen,* for what is seen is temporary, but what is unseen is eternal.
>
> (2 Corinthians 4: 16–18 NIV, emphasis added)

These scriptures shine a light on something so important in our walk of faith. It is where we *"fix our eyes"* in the hardships and battles which makes the difference between defeat and victory. If our faith is truly in God, we won't lose heart. We may not always feel on top of the world and occasionally experience brief moments of despair, but once discouragement attempts to take up residence, we will quickly kick it to the curb. When true faith in God is present a mature Christian will choose not to stay down and out.

⌒

Overwrought with despair, all I could think about was another wasted year filled with hospitals and pain. Barely eighty pounds and looking like a walking skeleton, thoughts of never being able to have children consumed me.

I soon grew strong enough to go home, but I did not want to leave the hospital in a gown. Without any one knowing, Dad decided to go shopping all by himself. He wanted to purchase something special for me to wear home. What he brought back caused quite a stir. It was a size one white jumpsuit, with "pit crew" and gas station names written across the pockets and sleeves, and a new pair of tennis shoes. No one could believe it! Robbie was the tomboy, I was the prissy one, but he beamed with excitement while everyone else chuckled. Not having the heart to say, *"Daddy, what were you thinking?"* I proudly wore it home, thankful to have such a loving father.

I left the hospital with some minor stomach pains but the doctors assured me they would pass. By the time we arrived home, it seemed the pains intensified with each passing hour and throughout the night Mom had to change my gown several times due to waking up completely wet from sweat. The next day I ran a high temperature as the pain continued. My parents called the doctor and he told them to bring me back to the hospital.

x-rays revealed adhesions throughout the abdomen wrapping around and blocking the intestines. This caused a serious bowel obstruction. Emergency surgery was done removing over six feet of adhesions and intestines. This seemed hard to believe considering my weight and size. The small intestine is about twenty feet long, and the large intestine is about five feet long. The human body and all its intricate details is quite amazing. It makes me wonder how anyone can doubt there is a God.

After a few days and noted improvement, I returned home. Surely nothing else could go wrong. If only this had been true. While lying on the couch and visiting with a friend I smelled a terrible odor and noticed my gown was wet around the incision area. My friend panicked and ran to get Mom and Dad. They checked my stitches and to our horror my stomach had burst open. Dad called the doctor, advising him of the situation. He suspected infection and possibly gangrene. All the way back to the hospital I cried and pleaded, *"God, please let me die, I can't take anymore!"*

We arrived at the hospital with everyone in tears. My parents could not console me and they were just as distraught. Only Jesus could deliver me out of this hell, but the only deliverance I wanted was death. Heaven held a much greater appeal than living one more minute on this earth.

As the surgeon entered the room I quickly informed him I was prepared to die and did not want another surgery. Taking my family out to the hallway, he advised them due to my state of mind and physical condition, putting me to sleep presented too many dangers. The doctors felt my only chance of making it through this ordeal meant doing the procedure with me fully awake. Although I faced a risk of going into shock, they felt certain I would never wake up from anesthesia. My poor parents reluctantly agreed and they proceeded without anesthetic.

I don't remember a lot about surgery except feeling intense pain and anger! Throughout the entire procedure, I pleaded with God to take me home. Tubes were everywhere, up the nose and down the throat with needles in my arms, neck, and chest. The tubes were pumping poison and infection out of my body and into large tanks that looked like scuba diving equipment. A large needle was stitched from the neck into my chest, administering some kind of medication to the heart. I can still recall how helpless I felt. If only I remembered what David said, *"When I am afraid, I will trust in You. In God, whose Word I praise, in God I trust; I will not be afraid, what can mortal man do to me?"* (Psalm 56:3, 4 NIV).

In and out of consciousness, the doctors prepared everyone for the worse. At one point, I remember waking up and seeing nothing but sad faces. Daddy looked as though he was a million miles away.

During times of consciousness, I could barely talk and if I did, the tubing crimped in my stomach, setting off all the alarms. To fix the tube the nurses had to bring it up, and then reinsert it back down the throat and stomach. The pain was excruciating. During this procedure, the needle in my chest had to stay completely still and in place. Mom often assisted the nurses by holding the needle and comforting me as they worked to fix the tube. There was a shortage of nurses during this time but with great compassion, everyone worked tirelessly to keep me alive, whether I wanted them to or not.

An amazing thing happened after one of these agonizing tube episodes. As pain gripped my body and I once again prayed to die, a beautiful figure appeared by the bed with a bright light shining all around. I immediately sensed this was an angel. An indescribable peace flooded my weary heart. The angel picked me in its arms, as we waded through what looked like a sea of infection and pollution. With a soothing calm the angel rebuked me for praying to die. It stated: *"Many children will pass through your arms and be blessed, there is still a work for you to do. You will not leave this earth until your work is complete."* My spirit stirred with humble appreciation and a shot of much needed faith. In spite of my angry and bitter heart, God still loved me enough to send a guardian angel to bring comfort and hope.

During times of unconsciousness, I could hear people talking. Nurses speculated about how long I would live, or if I'd make it through the night. Through it all, the angel stayed with me for a total of twenty-one days. In moments of discouragement when I wanted Mother, it spoke in a calm and soothing motherly voice. In times of fear and panic when I wanted Dad, it spoke in a strong and firm fatherly voice. Whatever I needed the angel became, whether it was a mother's gentle touch or a father's firm assurance.

The angel brought something else very special to the room. The entire time it stayed with me I only smelled a lovely fragrance of honeysuckle and vanilla. The smell of infection, gangrene, and medication disappeared. Everyday for three weeks it carried me in its arms, speaking scriptures of hope, blessings, and life:

. . . never will I leave you; never will I forsake you.

I can do all things through Christ which strengtheneth me.

Being confident of this, that He who began a good work in you, will carry it on to completion until the day of Jesus Christ.

My grace is sufficient for you, for my power is made perfect in weakness . . .

(Hebrews 13:5; Philippians 4:13; Philippians 1:5; 2 Corinthians 12:9)

The number of scriptures the angel spoke are too numerous to write. It still amazes me how loved I felt as the Word of God miraculously sustained me. Difficult obstacles lay ahead but thanks to this heavenly visitation, I knew God still loved me.

Psalm 91 is evidence God sends His angels to watch over and protect His children. In fact, my angel did exactly what is written in verse eleven.

> For He will command His angels concerning you to guard you in all your ways; *They will lift you up in their hands,* so that you will not strike your foot against a stone. You will tread upon the lion and the cobra; you will trample the great lion and serpent. Because he loves Me, say the Lord, I will rescue him; I will protect him, for he acknowledges My name. He will call upon Me, and I will answer him; I will be with him in trouble, I will deliver him and honor him. With long life will I satisfy him and show him My salvation.
>
> (Psalm 91:11–16 NIV, emphasis added)

CHAPTER 9

Daughter, Where Is Your Faith

We began questioning why so many things went wrong. Much to our dismay the information we received came a little late. Doctors recommended a radiation treatment after the hysterectomy because of scarring. We agreed to the procedure, not being informed of any serious side affects. An adverse reaction to the treatment created adhesions and scar tissue to rapidly form and wrap around my intestines. The result was a bowel obstruction, which caused the tissue to become infected and unable to heal. Before long, my stomach literally burst open with infection and gangrene.

Not being advised of the side affects, we were understandably upset and began asking why we were not informed. The doctors assumed the radiation dosage was too low for any complications, so they chose not to say anything. Too late to undo the damage, their assumptions proved wrong.

A month later, I walked out of the hospital with a huge hole in my stomach. To keep the wound free of infection the bandage had to be changed three to four times a day. They could not simply sew my stomach back up because it would burst open again causing more infection. The wound had to heal gradually from the inside, out.

The road to recovery grew even longer and more painful; however, I remained thankful for the caring people God placed in my life. The nursing staff became very dear to our entire family. The day I left the hospital, they presented me with a special pillow to use while recovering to prevent bedsores. Everyone signed the pillow with words of love and encouragement. They all commented about the special purpose God must have in store for me. They knew only a miracle brought me through this whole ordeal alive!

Years later I found myself thanking God for not answering my cries to end the misery and take me home. I am so glad I did not leave this world before experiencing the joy of walking in His abundant blessings while on this earth. The devil mistakenly counted me out, defeated, and broken. Praise God . . . *"I can do all things through Christ, for in my weakness He is strong!"*

Just to prove God cares about every little thing, before entering the hospital I felt a direct leading of the Holy Spirit to be financially responsible. God miraculously provided health insurance through work, but I did not want Mom and Dad burdened down with my bills. As a bank teller I took home about $400 a month; thankfully, my only debt was a car payment of $154.10, including insurance. After praying about it, I decided to pay my bills three months in advance. Between savings and checking, I had enough and mailed the advanced payments. Three months later, I returned to work making the next car payment on the fourth month, not even one day late. God truly cares about *every little thing!*

Mom and Dad were concerned about me going back to work with a hole in my stomach. Medication helped with pain management but changing the dressing at work presented a problem. I felt I could handle it, so I called my boss and asked her if I could come back. Demonstrating a great deal of patience and support, she welcomed me with open arms. Self conscious and terrified people might find out about the gaping hole, I asked her to keep my condition private and she kindly agreed.

Each day consisted of continuous pain and fatigue, but I refused to quit. Doctors made sure I was fully medicated at all times. This later became another obstacle to overcome. The enemy will use every means possible to destroy us.

I refer to the period from 1979 to 1985 as the "foggy years." The Lord must have been asking, *"Daughter, where is your faith?"* During this time doctors were so perplexed about my condition they simply wrote prescriptions for every symptom, pain, and infection. Not being able to find the source of my problems frustrated them terribly. Their answers or quick fixes usually came in the form of a pill or shot. Due to remaining heavily medicated throughout these years, it is amazing I functioned normally at all.

By the age of twenty, I was an emotional mess and felt worthless as a woman. Bob stayed on the roller coaster ride a long time, but he finally had enough. He could not take the constant pushing away and I did not blame him.

During our relationship, we talked about many things. I knew Bob longed for a little girl of his own one day, and I could never give that to him. His assurance of lasting love and God's ability to work things out did not matter. I remained stubborn and convinced being stuck with me would absolutely ruin his life forever. We maintained a tense friendship filled with sad regrets.

Desperately needing a change of scenery, I accepted a job offer in New Orleans. At the time, I thought makeup, a big smile, and stylish clothes hid everything; however, the truth has a way of rising to the surface. Wanting to experience some kind of normalcy, my parents hesitantly agreed to let me go. Extremely naïve, in poor health, and in a mental "la la land," I embarked on this new journey. My earthly possessions consisted of makeup, plenty of medication, and lots of pretty clothes.

Dad took me all over New Orleans trying to find a suitable place to live. I could not afford very much but he was determined to find a safe place, regardless of the cost. We soon found an adult only apartment complex complete with twenty-four hour security, and only a block from my job. Finding it hard to leave her baby, Mom stayed a few extra weeks to help me unpack and make sure I was okay.

When Mom left to go back home I quietly decided to take a "spiritual break." Thinking no one would ever know. I thought, *"Everyone needs a break from church and God at some point in their life, don't they?"* Satan loves it when we entertain these kinds of ideas, which often leads us to make really poor decisions.

Although God miraculously sent an angel to comfort and rescue me from death's door, seeds of bitterness and anger stayed harbored in my heart concerning the hysterectomy, no more Bob, years of pain, and over-all loss. Through it all, the Lord never stopped loving and protecting His little lost and hurting sheep. His love stayed unconditional and true.

> For I am with you and will rescue you...
> (Jeremiah 1:19 NIV)

After a few weeks of not attending church, I felt the Holy Spirit nudging, *"Donna, you should be in church. You need fellowship and more importantly, you need Me!"* Deciding to heed the nudge, I got dressed and went to a church located approximately fifteen minutes from the apartment. As I arrived, a young lady named Denise came over and welcomed me. Sensing my despair and being sensitive to the Holy Spirit, she became a loving and devoted friend. If I missed a service, Denise showed up at my door expressing concern and offering gentle encouragement.

One Sunday while the choir was singing, I felt overwhelmed with conviction. I could not run to the altar fast enough. Ashamed of how I blamed God for everything, He flooded me with His love and forgiveness as the anger melted away. What a wonderful Father! Denise stayed right by my side, praising God for answered prayer. Through obedience, she allowed herself to be instrumental in bringing me back to the Father.

A few months passed and another serious kidney infection set in. Just to keep going I increased the amount of pain medicine I took on a daily basis. Everyday I ran a high temperature while standing a straight eight to ten hours in high heels and swollen feet. The next thing I knew the bottom of my feet burst open. Unable to work and in desperate need of help left only one option, going back home. Feeling like a failure, I resigned my job and waited for Mom and Dad to come rescue their pitiful little girl.

They packed and moved me back home, immediately admitting me into the hospital. After a time of rest and recuperation, I went in search of a new job. God's hand of favor always shone through when I looked for employment. I did not withhold information regarding health issues, and yet I never experienced a problem finding work. Amazingly, prior employers gave good references in spite of my unpredictable attendance record. The only explanation for this is God's mercy and divine favor.

Receiving a job offer with Civil Service, I agreed to move to West Palm Beach for a ninety-day training period. After the ninety days, they offered to transfer me back home to one of the nearby military bases. Weighing about eighty-nine pounds and just getting over another major obstacle, I somehow convinced my parents I could handle it. Although they voiced many reservations they understood my intense desire to do something with my life, so they reluctantly loaded up the car and we headed South to find me a place to live.

Within a month, another serious infection hit and the doctors in West Palm immediately suspected leukemia. When the test results came back, just like all the doctors before them they realized it was incorrect, and they could not determine the problem either. The physician in charge was very kind and contacted Civil Service concerning the situation. The government notified us stating they would honor my time in West Palm, and allow the transfer to a local Base after my release from the hospital as agreed. The favor of God once again came to my rescue!

Upon my return, I received some unwanted news. Bob became engaged to someone he had been dating from a nearby church. I went to him in tears begging for another chance, but he could not risk the disappointment. Heartbroken, I tried to accept the fact he found happiness with someone else. The day of his wedding arrived feeling more like a funeral as I realized how foolish I had been and how empty my life would be without him.

The next four years I endured numerous hospitalizations, depression, and so much more. From 1979 to 1985, I honestly have very little recollection regarding many of the events that transpired. I considered writing about some of the situations, but most of the information is second hand. I cannot objectively write about things I only remember in parts and pieces. Some things are so painful I consider memory loss a blessing! In relationships, I made poor choices and suffered many things, including abuse. My state of mind was a spaced out, drug induced existence. By the grace of God I miraculously stayed employed, although I have very little memory of events or places.

Still feeling a call to ministry, I eventually forged ahead and enrolled in Bible School. I graduated with a "Specialized Ministry Diploma" with studies in youth, counseling, and music ministries. While working with Civil Service, (and a few years later, the State of Florida) I also received additional training and certification in the field of Mental Health. After a few more years, I continued my studies and pursued a Bachelor of Science Degree in Counseling Psychology and graduated Magna Cum Laude. God is a faithful and merciful Father!

Throughout these *"foggy years"* I discovered how cruel people with ulterior motives can be who prey on and take advantage of those who are weak and vulnerable. The saddest part, most of them were in the church. Through this experience, God stayed faithful and used the worst times of my life to teach me a lesson on loving others without judgment or condemnation; this continues to be a daily work in progress. When you have been wounded and hurt, it tends to make you more empathetic and caring to those in distress who have not led perfect lives.

In an effort to help others who have gone through or may be going through something similar, I want to use my situation as an example and take this opportunity to speak specifically to the church. Heaven knows I was messed up in every sense of the word, but all too often "Christians" turned to gossip and condemnation. In my particular situation, I am sure they felt fully justified, however, before reacting or responding we should ask the question, *"What is the loving thing to do?"*

Those who do not know Jesus are closely watching our lives. Many of the people gossiping and pointing a finger had no idea the amount of medication I took just to function and deal with the constant pain. They also did not consider the years of disappointment and torment involved from doctors running test after test trying to find answers and coming up with none. To make matters worse, having a hysterectomy so young created a severe hormone imbalance. Although I took monthly hormone shots my levels were never regulated, and I was anything but sane! Many years ago, they put women like me in asylums and sadly, I understand why.

We live in a world full of hurting, lost, and messed up souls who desperately need God. Many of these precious people will not darken the door of a church because of how we treat one another, while proudly calling ourselves *"Christians."* Being a Christian means Christ-like. It is not about making perfect choices, doing all the right things, or anything else. It is about loving people and bringing the lost to the knowledge of Christ.

When a brother or sister begins slipping and straying away from a Godly path, loving them does not mean ignoring the problem, but we must do as the Bible says:

> Brothers, if someone is caught in a sin, you who are spiritual should restore him gently. But watch yourself, or you also may be tempted. Carry each other's burdens, and in this way you will fulfill the law of Christ. If anyone thinks he is something when he is nothing, he deceives himself. Each one should test his own actions.
>
> (Galatians 6:1–4 NIV)

Everyone on the planet needs love and acceptance in spite of his or her dark circumstances. The lost need to know Jesus saves, heals, and beautifully restores what has been broken and shattered, regardless of who is to blame or how it happened. We must share the news in word and deed of a loving God who has a good plan for every one of us. He is not waiting to beat us over the head when we fail, instead, with love He longs to bring us back into the fold, using our situation to make us stronger and wiser.

We will talk about the issue of love and acting in love in a later chapter, but let's look at a commandment Jesus gave to ***all*** of us which must be put into practice every day we are on this earth. If we do as He commands, bondages will be broken, hearts will be mended, the wounded will heal, people will want to be a part of the Body of Christ, and miracles will manifest!

Jesus replied: "Love the Lord your God with all your heart and with all your soul and with all your mind." This is the first and greatest commandment. And the second is like it: 'Love your neighbor as yourself.'"

(Matthew 22:37–39 NIV)

When God called me into ministry, He knew the direction my life would take. He did not call me with plans to take it back because of mistakes and failures. We must remember *nothing ever takes Him by surprise.* One of my favorite scriptures is, *"For God's gifts and His call are irrevocable"* (Romans 11:29 NIV). This *Truth* offers comfort to those of us who have gifts and calls but have not walked a perfect path.

The years of uncertainty and confusion took its toll. Holding down a full time job proved difficult. To the bewilderment of many people including myself, employers were usually very good to me and I am forever grateful. God's favor is a wonderful thing.

During this time, I learned how creative, sovereign, slow to anger, and rich in mercy our Heavenly Father is, and how *He is more than able to reach across the heavens to bring compassion and love to one of His hurting kids.* If a willing vessel is nowhere to be found, He will find a way!

CHAPTER 10

His Mercies Fail Not

One October night in 1983 I came home from work very sick and headed straight for bed. Within hours, I began babbling and hallucinating due to a high temperature. My parents wrapped me in a blanket and took me to the hospital.

In the emergency room, visiting from Atlanta Georgia, was a doctor who *just happened* to be a liver and spleen specialist who came to town for a medical conference. He was using the emergency room computers to check on research data before heading back to Atlanta. As they wheeled me to a room, the staff began discussing my case. Because my symptoms sounded all too familiar to him, this visiting doctor joined in and started asking questions. Within moments, he asked for permission to do an examination, ordering additional tests and x-rays.

When the results came back, the doctor rushed into our room with x-rays in hand. He could not believe what he was seeing because my spleen was massively enlarged and my liver showed abnormalities as well. Bombarding us with questions, he asked, *"How long has she had this problem and who is treating her spleen?"* We had no answers; in fact, we did not even know this problem existed.

The doctor went into high gear giving out orders. He looked at my parents and stated, *"Her spleen has to be removed, and although her liver is enlarged this doesn't mean it is diseased, however, it's a sign of an underlying problem, which in this case I am sure has to do with the spleen. We must proceed quickly and make sure the liver is not damaged as well. If it is, we are looking at a very critical situation, but we will cross that bridge when and if we come to it. Pray for a miracle."* I can still recall how spellbound we were as he spoke. I said out loud to Mom and

Dad, *"Could it be possible someone has finally found out what has been wrong with me all these years? I can't take another disappointment, but this time something feels different."* My parents agreed. We all felt a flicker of hope.

It did not take long for all the test results to come back. They also requisitioned x-rays and charts from all my other doctors. After carefully reviewing reports from the previous eight years, dating back to 1975 (precisely when serious health problems began) all of the x-rays revealed an abnormally enlarged spleen. Fifteen at that time, my spleen was approximately three times the normal size with a slightly enlarged liver. Here we were eight years later and my spleen was significantly larger than the original report from 1975, and my liver was also abnormally enlarged.

When you have infection, it is not unusual for your spleen to enlarge slightly, however, year after year test showed a severe abnormality. In big letters all reports indicated, *"Enlarged spleen and liver, abnormality present!"*

Repeatedly, doctors pressed on my swollen side as I cried out in pain, yet continued to misdiagnose the problem. A few of them even believed it was psychological and psychosomatic. We soon found out their oversight resulted in unnecessary surgeries, physical internal damage, medications with harmful side affects, and just as devastating . . . tremendous emotional distress caused from the hysterectomy and years of suffering!

The Specialist requested to have me transported to Emory hospital in Atlanta. The spleen had to be removed and both the spleen and liver needed to be evaluated. After much discussion, he realized the hardship it would place on my family sending me six hours away. Dad could not simply pick up and leave town due to his many responsibilities. With this in mind, they called a surgeon from Pensacola, arranging for the operation to be performed there. This time I actually felt excited and relieved. Finally, there was a reason for all the years of pain. If my liver turned out okay, the prognosis looked good.

Our youth pastor started a prayer chain with churches near and far. Being in a military community many people came and went, so we had an extended family scattered around the globe. Thank God for praying Believers!

Surgery went well and best of all, my liver was not diseased. Praise the Lord for answered prayer. The surgeons were amazed at not only the size, but the condition of the spleen. They said I had been a walking time bomb for God only knows how long and could not imagine how I functioned on a day-to-day basis. They also discovered my hormone levels were horrendous. The doctor stated I should not be the least bit sane, and little did he know I had not been . . . Ha!

So many questions began to have answers once properly diagnosed and treated. The reason I threw up after every meal became clear. My stomach expanded for food, causing it to press against the enlarged and diseased spleen, setting off a cycle of problems resulting in pain, nausea, and vomiting. Mystery of misery finally solved!

The spleen produces antibodies and it removes old and abnormal red blood cells, platelets, and other damaged cells from circulation, reusing whatever parts it can. It also filters out bacteria and parasites from the blood and lymph that have been killed by white blood cells. A diseased spleen cannot filter these impurities properly and blood is seriously affected. The white cell count soars, as there is no longer the ability to fight off infection. Due to this, antibiotics only work temporarily as infections constantly attack the body. Another mystery solved!

Upon reading and learning the signs and problems of a dysfunctional spleen, I grew angry. For years my symptoms read word for word, right out of the medical journals. Examined and treated by so many physicians, it seemed incomprehensible no one correctly diagnosed the problem. I started asking some pretty tough questions: *"Why did I have to suffer for so many years and more importantly, could the hysterectomy have been avoided? And what about my hormones, wasn't it obvious to everyone I was a little batty? You would think a doctor with a nineteen- year- old patient who had a complete hysterectomy would keep an eye on her hormone levels, wouldn't you!"* My questions were never answered, but they sure made people nervous.

We never found out how (although we had our suspicions) but a well-known lawyer from Miami heard about my case and flew to Fort Walton for a consultation. He stated I would never have to work another day in my life if we allowed him to sue the doctors and hospitals. It sure sounded good, but something felt terribly wrong. How could I sue the doctors who tirelessly worked to keep me alive for so many years? Several of them truly agonized over my situation and desperately looked for answers. The cold hard truth stared me in the face, nothing and no amount of money could take away the suffering, or the pain of never having children. Choosing to trust God to bring justice to our cause, I decided against suing. My family completely understood and agreed with the decision. Memories of yesterday held too much pain. Only God could restore and bring healing, at least now I had hope!

After I made the decision, the Lord brought to light what actually transpired as Satan sought for years to destroy me. Just as God uses people and things, (whatever He desires) to carry out His plans, the enemy also uses anyone and anything to fulfill his schemes of destruction. I felt the Lord opened my eyes to see how the doctors were blinded by Satan and unable to see the problem. Yes, God is more powerful and could have removed the blinders; however, the *"why"* is not for me to ponder. Dwelling on *"what if"* is never constructive, and I had already lost too much valuable time consumed with sickness, hospitals, and unanswered questions. The fact is, God is God and I am not. He can do whatever He wants, however He chooses to do it.

Word spread like wild fire: *"Donna's not crazy; she's really had something wrong with her!"* Go figure! People began calling and apologizing for unkind things they had said or thought. Not understanding how to deal with my constant battle of sickness they found it easier to criticize, and like many of the doctors, speculated it must be psychological. In many ways I felt vindicated, but sad. I appreciated everyone's honesty and desire to make things right, but life seemed easier when I did not know what they thought. Then of course, there were the "foggy years" of which I had little recollection. What I could recall brought feelings of hurt, confusion, and tremendous shame.

To forgive others proved so much easier than forgiving myself. Have you ever wondered why that is? The answer is a carefully crafted plan of Satan to keep us beat down and unfruitful. When we forgive ourselves we are not consumed with self-pity and play-by-play regrets. It is very liberating. I knew what I had to do. Paul said it best.

> Forgetting what is behind and straining toward what is ahead, I press on toward the goal to win the prize for which God has called me heavenward in Christ Jesus.
> (Philippians 3:13–14 NIV)

Science has proven the affects of bitterness and unforgiveness are as devastating as any cancer or disease. For Believers, these things will kill the Spirit of the Living God that is alive within us and it grieves the Holy Spirit!

Learning to forgive myself would take time, but with determination and a restored hope I looked forward to a brand new beginning. I finally had the opportunity to plan for a new and healthier future.

Many challenges lay ahead. People suffering from chronic illness for prolong periods normally takes all kinds of medication on a regular basis, which can result in addiction. I, too, had fallen into this trap. Since doctors continued to write the prescriptions, I felt justified. That is called denial.

There were other complications too. I had scarring on my left kidney, and the doctors stated I would always experience problems with my nervous system because of all the surgeries and internal trauma caused by the diseased spleen. The results of these complications were occasional kidney infections, my blood pressure soaring high and dropping low, creating severe headaches and constant hand tremors.

One day I ran out of a store in tears, leaving everything on the checkout counter, because I could not stop shaking long enough to sign a check. Equally embarrassing was trying to hold a microphone when I sang in church. Every day living consisted of daily medications for pain, nerves, and blood pressure. Through the years, I simply learned to medicate and tolerate.

For some time I remained a broken and hurting young woman in need of complete healing and deliverance. It is hard to help others with any degree of success when you are a mess yourself. You cannot hide behind makeup, an outgoing personality, and fancy clothes forever . . . the truth will come out. With any addiction, (or obsessive behavior) honesty must be embraced in order to begin the process of healing. Only then can you become the Child of God you were meant to blossom into!

As the Holy Spirit brought healing and needed maturity to my mind, soul, and body, I realized how destructive certain past relationships had been and how I kept repeating a cycle of making the same mistakes over and over. My insecurities were numerous and out of control, causing me to look for love and fulfillment in people or things.

Wanting to be loved is natural, but if every relationship brings pain and abuse, something is wrong. *Stop and seek God for help!* We must be aware of something important; friends, mates, jobs, money, power, success—all these things and more—can become little idols we set up to make us feel better about ourselves or fill a void. This is not God's way nor does it lead to His best. *"Seek first the Kingdom of God, and all these things shall be added unto you."* In our impatience, we often seek *things* and try to add *the Kingdom* after the fact, and it does not work. Thankfully, God is *"slow to anger and rich in mercy."*

> It is of the Lord's mercies that we are not consumed, because His compassions fail not. They are new every morning; great is Thy faithfulness.
>
> (Lamentations 3:22, 23 KJV)

> Like a father pitieth his children, so the Lord pitieth them that fear Him.
>
> (Psalm 103:13 KJV)

But the mercy of the Lord is from everlasting to everlasting upon them that fear Him, and His righteousness unto children's children...

(Psalm 103:17 NIV)

CHAPTER 11

Challenges, Change and God's Amazing Grace

The next five years presented many challenges, changes, and a brand new Donna! In the midst of it all, the Holy Spirit remained faithfully at work mending and restoring all the past hurts. Addictions were broken and I could see the light of hope at the end of the tunnel.

One memory I could not shake had to do with Bob. I often wondered if anyone would ever make me feel as loved and accepted as I felt with him. By this time, we were no longer communicating and I missed my friend. I often slipped into the self-destructive world of *"what if."* Shaking those moments off, I forged forward but never stopped hoping the best for him and praying he was happy.

A few months after turning twenty-five, I met a nice Christian young man. He was stationed in the military and I invited him to our church. We discussed a mutual desire to be in a Christ-centered relationship and soon began dating. On our first night out he casually stated, *"I like kids, but I have no desire to ever have children of my own. I need to know how you feel about this."* Completely blown away, I proceeded to tell him about the hysterectomy and all the years I suffered with a spleen disease. That night I went home thinking, *"Okay Lord, this must be the person I am to marry. It won't bother him that I can't have kids. He'll accept me just the way I am."*

Convinced this was the hand of God, within nine weeks of our first date we became husband and wife. Whew! I suppose it would be an understatement if I said this is an area of my life that lacked maturity and Godly wisdom.

We married so quickly we did not take time for premarital counseling. I do not recommend this for anyone. My husband and

I barely knew one another and we assumed the *"Christian aspect"* would solve all our problems and make things great. Although we were terribly naïve, once we said *"I do"* we entered into a covenant with one another. More than anything, I wanted to be loved and happy so I determined to be the best wife possible, believing all my insecurities would somehow wash away!

Adapting to the military way of life presented many challenges. The downside, your spouse is frequently sent away on assignments for prolonged periods causing added stress and anxiety. The upside, the military provided total health care including medications for spouse and dependents. Being young and poor, this turned out to be a huge financial blessing.

I transferred all my health records to the base hospital and they assigned me a physician. My medical history intrigued the doctor and she showed a genuine interest in helping me overcome the constant tremors and headaches. They scheduled an MRI and CAT scan, hoping to reveal the specific areas of nerve damage. Consulting with a few of her colleagues, they decided to gradually wean me off pain and nerve pills and try a certain type of blood pressure medication used for controlling tremors and headaches, as well as blood pressure. Eventually the headaches and tremors were under control and for the first time in three years of marriage, my hands were steady and calm. When I sang, I could even hold a microphone without shaking. Hallelujah, restoration had begun!

During this time of restoration and hope, I received a disturbing letter from the hospital informing me there was a possibility of health problems associated with the blood I received from 1979 to 1983 during the hysterectomy, abdominal surgeries, and spleen removal. They requested I make an appointment for test as soon as possible because a large percentage of patients who received blood from the blood bank the hospital used at that time, came down with Hepatitis or the HIV/AIDS Virus. To make matters worse, during those years I received over nineteen units.

In 1979 and the mid to late 80's no one knew very much about the deadly AIDS virus, and scared does not begin to describe my state of mind. I made an appointment and received the necessary tests.

The results came back negative, but the doctor advised me to be tested every six months for the next five to ten years. Having survived so much already, we stood in faith and gave the situation to God. I continued being tested and God faithfully proved Himself powerful and mighty on my behalf.

Putting thoughts of Hepatitis or HIV/AIDS behind me and healthier now both mentally and physically, I felt strong enough to return to some form of counseling and finish what I started years prior. Although the Lord continued to bless my life, I was disappointed in the fact marriage did not *complete me* as a woman, or *fill the void.*

Instead of seeking God first for the best career path for my life, I decided I knew the answer and applied at counseling offices and mental health hospitals. My desire was to gain a sense of worth by helping those less fortunate and in distress.

An adolescent rehabilitation center offered me a position and I happily accepted. Day after day I witnessed the painful affects of abuse as I tried to help precious hurting children. Unable to simply close the door and leave it behind, I went home every day stressed out to the max. Still feeling empty and incomplete, confusion lingered followed by unanswered questions: *"Why isn't God blessing all my hard work? Why am I not happy?"* This works mentality continued to show up and rise to the surface. Despite these misguided efforts, God knew my heart and graciously showered me with His mercy and love. You see, at that time I failed to understand something important; the Lord rewards obedience, not good intentions, honorable professions, or anything else we can come up with to justify why we do what we do.

In a secular counseling setting, there are guidelines that must be adhered to when it comes to discussing Christianity. Although I was careful to obey the rules and regulations, God's amazing grace allowed me to be used whenever possible. As a Believer, I knew only Jesus could heal the hurt and remove the painful scars.

Back on the home front, tension brewed. When two people get married and begin a life together many adjustments must be made. Without careful consideration of one another, demands and selfishness will destroy intimacy and so much more in any relationship. With the *"honeymoon phase"* behind us, our marriage faced several huge obstacles. I was outgoing and very affectionate, while my husband felt uncomfortable showing affection and preferred to stay home. My idea of a good time consisted of walks, talks, movement, and action while he was content to sit by himself in front of the computer for hours, with occasional conversation and limited togetherness.

Instead of understanding the dynamics of how to build a healthy relationship and work with one another's differences, we complained, accused, and failed to learn how to spend quality time together. We were busy doing the right things like going to church and helping those in need, but *"doing or working"* for the Lord and *"walking the love walk"* are two very different things. To complicate matters, we were leaving out the very one who possessed the wisdom and guidance we desperately needed to make our marriage happy and healthy ...Jesus!

Hoping to reduce stress at home, I resigned from the hospital and accepted a new position in an adult assisted living facility. These particular patients suffered with a wide range of mental health issues, including abuse and addiction challenges. It did not take long to realize this change did not meet my expectations. Stress and tension continued at home. I suppose we were like most married couples, tolerating one another with occasional moments of laughter and love.

Several years passed along with burn out and frustration before realizing, *"Hey Donna, don't you think this career choice is a big mistake? You are much too sensitive and way too emotional for this kind of work."* Finally, the lights came on!

I admire the brave souls in the mental health field who dedicate their lives to these professions. It takes a special person with a true calling to face the human suffering they see on a daily basis. At the end of the day you have to leave it behind, go home, and balance a healthy and happy relationship with spouse and family.

I do not believe God had this path in mind when He designed me. I am *"the glass is half full"* kind of gal, who loves to laugh and just enjoy the fact I am alive! For so many years I had to encourage myself of the possibility of tomorrow, and being around negativity and constant problems makes me physically sick. It honestly takes a toll on my body, mind, soul, and spirit. Any self-respecting counselor will tell a person of this nature not to pursue the mental health, rehabilitation, or abuse fields. Of course, if someone had tried to tell me I probably would not have listened. In the meantime, the on-going desire to minister and reach out to hurting people sent me in many directions, just not the right ones.

Before long, my husband received orders to Germany for a two-year tour. Due to a lack of civilian medical facilities, military doctors recommended I remain in the States because of the frequent bladder and kidney infections I continued to have. Not wanting to be alone and needing to save money, I moved back home. Giving up some independence was difficult but I enjoyed being with Mom and Dad. Once the baby, always the baby!

A number of things transpired before my husband's departure sending feelings of inadequacy and insecurities spiraling out of control. Sadly, I actually sighed with relief when he left. I am sure he felt the same way. Longing for the blessings of God, we sought forgiveness from one another, but dividing walls remained. We corresponded by letters and phone calls, in an effort to work out our problems and give each other support. When Christ is no longer "Lord" of your home, Satan has a stronghold that can destroy everything and anything good remaining.

Throughout the years, I have observed a number of things regarding relationships. Some of the wisdom I have obtained is a direct result of my own failures; others are by examples and revelations. One critical issue seems to be the desire to feel important, needed, and whole. A close and continual relationship with Jesus Christ is the only thing that can bring anyone a sense of acceptance and wholeness. Our mates, family, children, or careers only define a portion of who we are; however, they cannot complete us, fill every void, or right every wrong. To demand this places unrealistic expectations on ourselves, and everyone around us. It also causes strife and unnecessary emotional pain. Marriages and families are torn apart and destroyed every single day due to selfishness, insecurities, regrets from the past, wrong motives of the heart, and unrealistic expectations.

Pride is usually the source of these issues. When we refuse to humble ourselves to our God, our mates, or anything that prevents us from *"having it our way,"* we should pay close attention to the scripture, *"Pride comes before downfall."* When we find ourselves *demanding our rights* and *unwilling to bend*, pride is definitely rearing its ugly head and we are no longer acting in love. Too often, we fail to recognize what love should sound or look like because it interferes with *getting our own way* or *our agenda*. I am not proud of this, but I regularly responded in ways love *is not*, and a downfall was inevitable.

So, where do we find the guidelines for love? I believe the following scriptures clearly define love and its behavior. As you read them, make the decision today to be *"hearers"* and *"doers"* of the Word!

> Love is patient, love is kind. It does not envy, it does not boast, it is not proud. It is not rude, it is not self-seeking, it is not easily angered, it keeps no record of wrongs. Love does not delight in evil, but rejoices with the truth. It always protects, always trusts, always hopes, always perseveres. Love never fails.
>
> (1 Corinthians 13:4–8 NIV)

CHAPTER 12

Friends and Farewells

After a year apart, my husband and I made plans to meet in his hometown in upstate New York for Christmas. We were together three weeks, but stayed with his parents the entire time. Although they were kind and gracious, it was difficult and awkward, with very little privacy. Another year would pass before we saw one another again.

Back at home, I took comfort in work, daily reading the Bible, and volunteering in the music and youth department at Dad's church. Before long, the Lord opened an unexpected and wonderful door of opportunity, in the form of a friend.

One Sunday morning a beautiful young woman visited our church. She was tall and thin with long flowing dark hair. As the service ended, she made her way to the front and rededicated her life back to God. At one time she served the Lord, but like so many of us allowed circumstances and painful experiences to turn her away.

After praying you could physically see a transformation in this young woman. The scripture, " . . . *old things are passed away; behold, all things are become new*" became so real to me when she rose to her feet. She looked like a completely different person, a brand-new creation!

My new friend shared with me how her husband left their marriage and she struggled with the pain of divorce and losing someone she deeply loved. The process of divorce is never easy, regardless of the circumstances or who is to blame.

As our friendship and strong bond of trust continued to develop, we visited daily, shared laughter and tears, and studied the Bible together. A safety net surrounded us like a shield, allowing the most intimate feelings and thoughts to be exposed. During this time of discipleship the Lord began to manifest the gift of discernment in my life. It was a strange but wonderful experience.

Many of us carry around scars and memories of past hurts. They seem too great to bear, and too devastating to share with anyone. My friend kept one of these painful secrets closely guarded and tucked away. God gently waited, longing to heal the hurt in her heart and abundantly restore all the things Satan stole from her life.

One night we attended a Christian concert. The singer began sharing a testimony when the Lord spoke something directly to me concerning my friend. It felt as if God Himself sat down beside me and whispered in my ear. An overwhelming love and compassion consumed every cell of my being. I felt this young woman needed assurance of the Father's unconditional and unrelenting love for her; and before I realized it I leaned over and said, *"God not only loves you, but He desires to heal and restore your broken heart and life. His love is without boundaries or conditions, and He is about to reach past your mistakes and failures and give you a miracle. He is not angry, you are His daughter and He truly loves you!"* Grabbing her by the hand and putting my arms around her, we walked outside to the parking lot. With the anointing of the Holy Spirit I shared an intimate and painful issue God showed me about her past. It was something I had no way of knowing. We stood for a moment shaking and broken before the Lord. Feeling an unbelievable joy, we clung to one another in praise and gratitude for God's forgiveness, healing, and restoration.

Heading back to her house our praise continued past midnight into the early morning hours. After that night she would never be the same. Standing in awe of God's mercy and the humbling power of the discerning Holy Spirit, I too felt a sense of renewal and expectation.

> No, in all these things *we are more than conquerors through Him who loved us.* For I am convinced that neither death nor life, neither angels nor demons, neither the present nor the future, nor any powers, neither height nor depth, nor anything else in all creation, will be able to separate

us from the love of God that is in Christ Jesus our Lord.
(Romans 8:37–39 NIV, emphasis added)

If reading this story brings up unresolved issues in your own life that have been carefully tucked away in a secret corner of your heart, let me encourage you to turn those things over to Jesus *today* for He alone has the power to heal and miraculously restore. Christ tells us to come to Him and He will give us rest. There is a miracle of healing waiting for you right now. The only way to receive it is to give everything over to the Heavenly Father. His arms are open wide waiting for you to run in and find rest!

> Come to Me, all you who are weary and burdened, and I will give you rest. Take My yoke upon you and learn from Me, for I am gentle and humble in heart, and you will find rest for your souls. For My yoke is easy and My burden is light.
> (Matthew 11:29, 30 NIV)

My husband returned home from Germany with orders to Plattsburgh Air Force Base in New York. We felt peace about the assignment and prayed it would give us the opportunity to focus on one another without many distractions. Saying goodbye to family and friends would be difficult but life must go on. After a river of tears and sad farewells, we left Florida, anxious and excited about the future.

Upstate New York is beautiful, but definitely cold. The colors and changes of the seasons left me speechless. Then the snow came . . . Wow! I may have been thirty but I bundled up like a kid and played outside for hours. Florida beaches are gorgeous, but this topped anything I had ever seen.

Before being assigned permanent housing, we lived in temporary quarters for about thirty days. As soon as we settled in, I began looking in the yellow pages for churches focused and determined to get on track and stay there.

My husband never said much about his time in Germany; however, he did mention there were numerous Bible study groups but few churches. He casually stated he did not regularly attend either one. This information scared me and presented a big problem in our already troubled marriage.

I am not talking about legalism. We are not saved by the law, but Satan is cunning and deceptive. When we stop meeting together in fellowship we open ourselves up to temptation and so much more. We often wonder why certain sins have come upon us, when we are slow or slothful in being faithful to the things that keep us strong and accountable. Even when we fail miserably, if with a pure heart we stay *faithful to the things of God*, He will come to our rescue with wisdom and direction; placing us firmly back on our feet.

Over the years my failures were too many to count, but had I not been in church and stayed in fellowship with Believers, the road back would have been longer and filled with additional challenges to overcome.

As Christians, we are free to serve from a heart of love and obedience. God does not reward those who attend church regularly out of obligation, or with ulterior and wrong motives; however, His Word says He rewards the *faithful*. One definition of *faithful* is, "true to one's word, promises, or vows." Being *good stewards* of all God has blessed us with, and *faithfulness* is of utmost importance to the Father. Knowing this, we should examine our priorities and honestly admit why we choose to not heed and obey God's Word. Scripture tells us, *"The little foxes spoil the vine."*

My husband and I made a promise to find a place of fellowship and stay faithful, both agreeing this must be a priority in our home. The next step would be honoring our commitment and being obedient.

As time passed, I found myself daily reorganizing, cooking, and cleaning like a woman possessed. Bored from not enough to do, I needed a job and a reason to get up. With only one vehicle, I had to find something to do from home or on the military base.

While grocery shopping one afternoon I saw a sign in the commissary window advertising for Home Daycare Providers. This would enable me to work with children in a positive way, without all the heartbreaks. My husband agreed and seemed delighted with the decision. I filled out the paperwork, took the classes, and received my certification. Before long, I enrolled two babies and three, three-year-olds.

These children became my very own extended family. Sensing my loneliness and need for companionship, their parents included me in outings and activities. They were wonderful people, willing to share their lives and children. As marital woes grew more intense, the love I received from these families helped lessen the moments of depression.

In an effort to be fair regarding our deteriorating marriage, I want to express the fact we both bore the responsibility of what happened. Desperately wanting to be a mother, I stayed wrapped up with the children, while my husband chose to hide away in the computer room for hours on end. Tired of struggling, we learned to tolerate and accept this existence we called marriage. We were both in the wrong and acted selfishly.

Two years passed and my little ones were growing more every day. While busy planning a birthday party for one of them, I received a phone call from home. Dad and Mom were both on the line, but Dad said something I could not believe, *"Baby, Mamas been diagnosed with Lymphoma cancer and they found a number of tumors, can you come home?"* Mom tried to sound strong and tough, but I knew her all too well. I told them I would get packed and be home just as soon as I could get a plane ticket.

Like many mothers and daughters, we often clashed during my teenage years. Our struggles with constant illness created a bond *and* division throughout childhood and adolescence. The main reason for the tension had to do with the fact we were undeniably so much alike. After the hysterectomy, something changed between us. I needed Mom's strength just to keep sane, and this dependency created a strong and unshakable friendship. I could tell her anything and it seemed as though she saw right into my heart. At the same time, Mom confided in me. Being a pastor's wife is often challenging and she could not open up to just anyone. It was an honor to be her daughter and her friend.

Our parents always gave us their unconditional love and support. Now it was our turn to be there for them. Numb and unable to process a rational thought, I hung up the phone, dropped everything, and began packing. To this day, I cannot remember what happened to the birthday party I planned.

I said goodbye to my sweet babies and their families, knowing I would miss them terribly. The military granted my husband a humanitarian assignment back home. He stayed in Plattsburgh an additional thirty days to process, pack, and move.

What happened next is best described as God's amazing grace in action. I took a ferry to Vermont and boarded a small plane enroute to a larger airport. Thoughts of how hopeless cancer sounded and the possibility of losing Mother weighed heavily on my mind. I sat in my seat praying, when a man touched my hand and said, *"Hi, my name is Mr. Pillsbury, is there anything I can do?"* The compassion and love of Jesus shone in his eyes as he offered to pray with me. I quietly thought, *"God, is this another angel?"* A flood gate of emotions broke and I proceeded to sob and tell him the whole story. At that very moment I knew God sent him to soothe my hurting heart, a real flesh and blood angel. Thank you Father!

The miracle of this meeting soon became clear to both of us. He recently flew to this small remote town in Vermont to visit with his elderly mother and was on his way home to Florida . . . Fort Walton Beach to be exact! God is so awesome. Never leaving my side, we shared the same flight schedule and connections giving us the opportunity to pray and talk, as well as enjoy some much-needed moments of laughter.

During a layover, I called home to check in and Mom answered the phone. She tried to sound upbeat, but I could tell she was scared. I hung up sobbing uncontrollably. Mr. Pillsbury rushed toward me with arms opened wide. *God knew just how to get His arms of love around me. He is such a good Father.*

Home at last, we entered the airport where my family awaited. Introducing my new friend, we shared the sequence of events that brought us together as everyone rejoiced. We said goodbye and promised to stay in touch.

Several months later Mr. and Mrs. Pillsbury surprised me by popping in to one of our services. Meeting Mrs. Pillsbury for the first time, I realized she possessed the same spirit of compassion and love as her husband. The Family of God is a glorious thing.

Over the next four months, marital woes took a back seat. Unable to feel any emotion concerning our relationship, I became the ultimate caretaker and devoted all my time and energy to Mother.

CHAPTER 13

Mama Says Hello to Jesus

Chemotherapy is a word I learned to dislike. Doctors gave us facts and information; however, they could not predict how Mom's body might tolerate the treatments. We were given two scenarios, one good and one bad. They felt optimistic as long as no serious complications occurred. Her overall health seemed to be the greatest concern. In times past, Mom always said she'd refuse chemotherapy if faced with cancer, but to our surprise she chose to take it. Seeming at peace with her decision, we pressed forward into the unknown. We knew God could heal her with or without chemo, so we did the best and only thing we knew to do . . . *Pray for a miracle!*

Mom talked about heaven a lot during this time. One day she looked at me and said, *"I want you to know I am looking forward to meeting Jesus face to face; and just think baby, I'll never have another day of pain, pills, and suffering."*

The next four months the family took every opportunity to spend time with Mom. We laughed, cried, and shared stories of days gone by. She did not sleep well at night, so Dad slept on the other side of the room where he studied, and I slept on an egg crate next to her bed. We talked privately for hours during the night about her concerns and the dreams she had for each one of us.

Dad and I were the primary caretakers. Robbie lived a few hours away and her son Chad was in junior high school, but they came home often. Larry, Judy, and Amanda lived in town and helped as much as they could. Judy worked full time, yet never failed to be available with a helping hand and words of encouragement. Amanda and Chad lavished their granny with lots of love and she enjoyed the attention and time they gave her.

My parents loved each other deeply. Mother was only fifteen when they married and Dad had become her everything. In sickness and in health, the good times and bad, they were truly there for one another.

Although Mother battled sickness most of her life, she always found a way of bringing humor and hope to our home. She was a firecracker in every sense of the word and people loved being around her. Her infectious laugh reverberated like a chain reaction, and when Mama laughed everyone joined in!

Dad's desperation over her illness grew with each passing day. Suffering with high blood pressure and heart problems, mounting stress caused him to suffer a mild stroke. We always saw Dad as the rock, but soon realized Mama was the emotional glue holding things together.

God mercifully intervened and he made a full recovery. On the funny side, during the stroke Dad made several wacky and strange comments. Mama spent the next month advising him and everyone else, *"It finally happened, Edward lost his ever lovin' mind!"*

My failing marriage concerned Mom. Constant reassurance from me did not sway her from worrying. We were living in her home and she saw first hand the lack of affection and indifference. We basically lived separate lives. Mom also understood the painful void I felt from not having children. When I lived in New York, we spent hours talking on the phone and laughing about all the things *"my babies"* got into. My husband and I discussed adoption but he could never make the commitment. Our desires for a family were very different. I eventually reconciled myself to the fact adoption was not an option, case closed. Knowing all of this, Mama never stopped praying for us. During her illness she shared many personal and prophetic things with me. In time, every one of them proved to be true.

Christmastime soon arrived. Decorations, lots of presents, and the smell of turkey and dressing filled the house. Everyone sensed this might be our last Christmas with Mom. More tumors were found and the doctor intensified the treatment. She was so frail and weak, but somehow mustered up the strength to play the piano. We all gathered in the living room to sing and praise God. As we exchanged presents, we knew that having Mother with us was a precious gift, and we would be forever thankful for this special time together.

Later that night Mom made an unexpected request, she wanted my sister and me to sing at her funeral. Pleading with her to reconsider, she refused to hear any excuses. Mom stated she did not want anyone ruining her favorite songs at her very own funeral. Robbie and I knew exactly what she meant. She did not like it when singers failed to pronounce their words properly or sang too nasally. Mama always said, *"When you sing for the Lord you should do your very best, and for heaven's sakes, don't sound like you're whining!"* We wanted to grant her request, but how? Mom was 4'10" and barely ninety pounds (even less with the cancer) but make no mistake about it, she always had the final say and it was in your best interest to listen!

My sister and I were in our teens before Mom received healing for her kidneys. Growing up, simple every day task proved difficult for her because of pain and infection, but she refused to allow anything to keep us from getting to our music lessons. The ultimate perfectionist, she worked long hours every week teaching us the importance of giving God our best when we sang or played the piano. She made us practice over and over again saying, *"Girls, you can't bless someone with the words of a song if they can't hear or understand what you are saying. If you're gonna do it, do it right!"*

Mom imparted her love and gift of music to us, and although we failed to appreciate it at times, we loved her dearly for it. Knowing this, we would have to find the strength to sing at her funeral should Jesus choose to take her on to heaven.

Things took a turn for the worse on January 1, 1994. Mom started having trouble breathing. Fearing the onset of pneumonia, we rushed her to the hospital. The drive felt like an eternity as every breath grew harder for her to take. When we arrived and wheeled her in the emergency room, she began gasping for air. She always said she never wanted to be on life support, but turning critical so fast; Dad only had seconds to make the decision. Before we realized it, doctors and nurses were hooking her up to tubes and machines. Feeling this would be temporary, we all prayed she understood.

Things continued happening way too fast. We were not ready to let Mama go. How do you prepare to lose someone you love? We all felt like robots just going through the motions of walking and breathing.

Afraid to leave the hospital, we slept in the waiting room for seven days. We only left one time to get a change of clothes. January 7, 1994 the family stood around Mom's bed hand in hand, singing in harmony her favorite songs. While we sang, Mama slipped into the arms of Jesus. In the natural, we wanted to fall apart but the mercy and comfort of the Holy Spirit held us together.

Dad walked around in a daze. His wife and best friend for over fifty years was gone. Only the good Lord could sustain him through this. Going through the motions, we proceeded to do all the things you are supposed to do when a love one dies. By the grace of God we were able to sing at the funeral and make it through without breaking down.

Mom received the ultimate healing—never again to suffer pain, sorrow, or sickness. What a glorious thought. It would be selfish to want her back. One day we will see her again, and what a reunion that will be! Thoughts of heaven are more wonderful because she is there. Mama truly left a mark and legacy of love.

Her death brought about many changes. After over fifty years of faithful ministerial service to the Lord and thirty-two of those years spent at Wright Assembly, Dad announced his retirement.

With Dad retiring and Mom gone, I felt lost. I continued to attend church but my communion with the Lord grew cold. I wanted a change and could no longer tolerate things that were wrong in my life by simply ignoring them. My husband and I agreed to seek Christian counseling and made an appointment.

A number of things came out during counseling, which would have been very beneficial to know before getting married; however, it gave us an understanding on why we had so many difficulties. It appeared the majority of our problems had to do with issues from the past and childhood trauma. Painful things were revealed and dealing with them would not be easy. Unsuccessful in our efforts and tired of struggling, I wanted out. After almost ten years of marriage, we divorced.

Not long after the divorce, we met together and asked each other for forgiveness. We walked away that day sad but thankful. We knew according to scripture we must be willing to forgive if we expected God to forgive our sins.

God's will is not divorce; however, if we will repent and humble ourselves before the Lord, He will forgive and bring restoration. Divorce is not an unpardonable sin.

> For if you forgive men when they sin against you, your heavenly Father will also forgive you. But if you do not forgive men their sins, your Father will not forgive your sins.
> (Matthew 6:14, 15 NIV)

I desperately wanted God's forgiveness and no one or nothing is worth dying and going to hell over. Once again, I allowed shame and condemnation to keep me from forgiving myself. I continued to wonder, *"How many more mess-ups will God allow before He slaps me into eternity?"*

In time and with the help of the Holy Spirit, my life would make a dramatic and lasting change. God planned to restore and resurrect things I assumed were forever buried, *"His gifts and call."* In the process, teach me a valuable lesson on the joy and freedom of forgiving one's self!

CHAPTER 14

Church, Hypocrites and Forgiveness

Using the Bible as a guide, I want to discuss church, hypocrites, and forgiveness. Jesus is very direct when it comes to these matters. It will point toward the *Truth* of God's Word, and offer instruction on how to live together in love and harmony.

Let me clarify something, this is not about a building. It is about the "Family of Believers," which includes the church, missions, cell groups, house churches, wherever we come together in unity and fellowship professing *"Christianity."*

The entire Body of Christ desperately needs Godly wisdom in dealing with "sin issues" such as divorce, abuse, homosexuality, pre-marital sex, and many more life altering challenges. These issues lead to disease, pregnancy, emotional scarring, and all different levels of brokenness. People need our love and encouragement, not condemnation and additional wounds.

Statistics show Christians have as hard of a time forgiving one another as Unbelievers therefore, we cannot ignore those within the *family* who continue to condemn people to hell, humiliate, and shoot our wounded. There are entirely too many souls lost and dying without Christ because of witnessing the unloving ways we have treated one another, all in the name of the Lord. This must break the Father's heart. It is no wonder we are not seeing miracles and souls saved in our local churches on a grander scale. The world does not want what we have and who can blame them!

Every year the number of people leaving the church increases at an unbelievable rate because they cannot find the support and acceptance they are in desperate need of. This is wrong and we must change! Jesus Christ is the *only* lasting answer to the hurts of this world. Although the Bible tells us to hate the sin, *we must love the sinner. This is not a cliché, it is Truth!*

Every man, woman, and child has value and worth in God's Kingdom. It is not our job to decide who is worthy of His mercy and forgiveness. We must repent, turn from our wicked ways, and serve in love; staying focused on our mission according to scripture, *"All this is from God, who reconciled us to Himself through Christ and gave us the ministry of reconciliation"* (2 Corinthians 5:18 NIV). The *"ministry of reconciliation"* means to reach the lost so that they can be reconciled to Jesus Christ, and restore the wounded back to the Savior.

On a positive note, we have seen and heard of churches throughout America offering divorce, abuse, and other kinds of care and counsel necessary for a healthy over-all wellbeing and after some research, I discovered these programs are on the rise. I pray they continue to increase in number and wisdom.

Jesus illustrates compassion for His children and their worth in the Kingdom with the Parable of *"The Lost Sheep."* Our Creator, the Savior of the world set the example for us. Who are we to show any less compassion for the lost and hurting than He did!

> But if anyone causes one of these little ones who believe in Me to sin, it would be better for him to have a large millstone hung around his neck and to be drowned in the depths of the sea.
>
> (Matthew 18:6 NIV)

> See that you do not look down on one of these little ones. For I tell you that the angels in heaven always see the face of My Father in heaven. What do you think? If a man owns a hundred sheep, and one of them wanders away, will he not leave the ninety-nine on the hills and go look for the one that wandered off? And if he finds it, I tell you the truth, he is happier about the one sheep than about the ninety-nine that did not wander off. In the same way your Father in heaven is not willing that any of these little ones should be lost.
>
> (Matthew 18:10–14 NIV)

Notice He says, *"But if anyone causes one of these little ones who believe in Me to sin. . . ."* He is referring to *"His sheep"* or *"children in the faith,"* not an Unbeliever. This parable is about the hurting, the misguided, the lost . . . Whatever the label, it is about those of us who believe, but tragically get off track.

Ask yourself, *"Do I receive or despise others? Do I judge or encourage? Does my attitude cause others to stumble or does it edify and offer hope?"* Meditate on these questions and ask the Holy Spirit to reveal areas in your heart and life that are not Christ-like. Be prepared to repent and turn from walking a selfish and destructive path.

Now let's talk about one of the most popular reasons individuals leave the church—hypocrisy. Yes, it is a legitimate problem but there are just as many hypocrites outside the church as there are inside. So, what is the difference between the ones inside and those outside? First of all, Believers should know better. Scripture tells us we are to be a *"peculiar people"* who are *"hearers and doers"* of the Word, consistently putting *"love"* into action. So why don't we? If you asked my opinion, I would say pride.

From Genesis to Revelation, pride appears to be a main root of sin. Some may argue the *"fear of man"* is the problem, however, when we fear doing right because of another person's response, we are actually exalting them above God. Webster's dictionary describes pride as, *"a high opinion of one's self, person, or object."* So we should ask ourselves this question, *"Whose opinion should matter, God our Creator, or man, His creation?"* The only way to resolve this issue is to put into practice what the Bible says, *"Demolish arguments and every pretension that sets itself up against the knowledge of God, and we take captive every thought to make it obedient to Christ"* (2 Corinthians 10:5 NIV).

Because of pride, we are afraid to be *"real"* causing us to put on a *"false face."* We tend to judge and criticize others trying to hide our own shortcomings, thus, becoming a hypocrite. Somehow, we fool ourselves into believing no one sees us as we truly are. You might fool a few people for a short time, but eventually the *truth* will rise to the surface.

Writing this book challenged me in this area. Being "real" meant telling many painful, pitiful, and stupid things about my life. Reading about the mistakes I repeated over (and over) again probably made you think, *"Man, this chick really needs to get a clue,"* and I agree! Remembering all the sordid details made me feel the same way; however, my heart's desire was to get my love walk right between God and man.

Those who are serious about their love walk will tell the *truth* at the risk of ridicule, gossip, and shame. They will humbly *"reveal all"* for the sake of forgiveness and saving someone else from pain and suffering. This is where a hypocrite parts ways with a *genuine* Believer. They cannot risk this kind of exposure. It is more important for them to continue in deceit and denial than *truth* and *love.* On the other hand, a *genuine* Christian will hold tightly to the fact they are washed in the blood of the Lamb and 100% forgiven. Receiving and not letting go of God's *Truth* enables us to be *vulnerable, sincere, fruitful, and real . . . The Truth shall set you free!*

Those within the church who suffer from a *"works mentality"* usually gravitate toward the life of a hypocrite. They often ignore the issues and focus on working their way into the Kingdom, and eventually wear themselves out. Too tired from *"doing"* but not *"hearing,"* they become cranky, tired, judgmental, and unfulfilled. Many times you will see the negative results within the dynamics of their family life. I know about this, for many years I was one of these misguided souls.

In conclusion of the "hypocrite" subject, let's look at how this affects the Body of Christ . . . The Church. Unfortunately, as long as there are people there are problems. Hypocritical behavior can manifest in many different ways. The behaviors I see acted out most frequently are gossip, critical spirits, harboring bitterness and unforgiveness, and people's words not matching their actions.

So, what do we do when *"Brother or Sister Loose Lips"* mistreats, judges, or even falsely accuses? Moreover, what do we do when someone hurts us in painful ways of which we are not at fault? These can be difficult questions, especially when you are a victim of unjust actions and motives.

Regardless of the sin or situation, the scripture is clear. If we do not forgive, we will not be forgiven. Is this fair? Not always. Is it the right thing to do? Always. So why don't we? It boils down to a *choice* and only you and God can answer this question.

One thing to keep in mind is this, *forgiving is not forgetting or even trusting.* There are painful experiences many of us have endured of which we will never forget; however, the *power of forgiving* causes anger and bitterness to flee. Memory can serve as a testimony of God's restoration power, as well as to help others who are suffering. When past hurts replay in your mind, offer praise to God for what He has brought you through, and with determination resist feelings of bitterness, condemnation, and anger.

Depending on the situation, trusting the individual (or individuals) we have forgiven is not always an option or even wisdom, but with the help of the Holy Spirit and God's amazing grace, we can be overcomers and walk in love. Ask the Holy Spirit for help as you apply forgiveness and *stay in the Word!* It will sustain you and lead your feet down a path that promotes a growing, liberating, and healthy love walk.

If you are struggling in this area, make a decision today to *hear* the Word, *receive* the *Truth,* and with the help of the Holy Spirit *become* a *"Doer."* It is a freeing experience to walk in forgiveness, filled with peace and joy.

> For if you forgive men when they sin against you, *your heavenly Father will also forgive you. But if you do not forgive men their sins, your Father will not forgive your sins.*
> (Matthew 6:14, 15 NIV, emphasis added)

Allow me to bring one important point to the forefront before moving on. A sobering fact is this; if we do not forgive, we will spend eternity in hell with the very hypocrites we despise so badly! This is not my opinion it is God's Word. When we pray, we cannot harbor bitterness and unforgiveness toward *anyone,* because it will close the ears of God and hinder His ability to forgive us. You see, God does not change, He does not lie, and He abides by His Word. If we do not forgive neither will He, and no sin will be permitted in heaven. Our choices are quite simple, heaven or hell.

When I reflect back on the forgiveness God has extended toward me, it becomes abundantly clear my response must always be to forgive! Make a decision today to serve the Lord in love, striving to do the right thing regardless of anything or anyone else. Ask the Holy Spirit to reveal any areas of pride or bitterness in your heart, then be willing to *repent* and *choose Truth*. Doing this will create a powerful love walk and you will become much more fruitful for the Kingdom of God.

Pray for the Body of Christ as a whole. If you are not currently attending a church, ask God to lead you to a fellowship you and your family can call home with a shepherd who has a heart for discipleship, instructing and teaching God's Word in *Spirit* and *Truth*. Choose to become a vessel of hope, love, and compassion to those inside and outside the Church. Become part of the solution, not the problem.

> If My people, who are called by My name, will humble themselves and pray and seek My face and turn from their wicked ways; then will I hear from heaven and will forgive their sin and heal their land.
>
> (2 Chronicles 7:14 NIV)

No one knew better than Jesus and me how off the mark my life had drifted. Mercifully, God heard my cries of genuine repentance. I did not deserve His forgiveness but He freely gave it. For too many years I failed to receive this precious gift, hindering God's blessings in my life and thus limiting His ability to use me to the fullest for His glory. Although I will never get back those wasted years, I believe by sharing my story someone's eyes will be enlightened to the *Truth*. *Make a choice today* to forgive yourself and others and walk in freedom, no longer bound by shame and condemnation.

The Bible tells us, *"Therefore there is now no condemnation for those who are in Christ Jesus"* (Romans 8:1 NIV). The time is *now*. Jesus Christ has set us free from the bondage of sin. If I had made all the right decisions and never strayed, I would ***not*** be considered a more worthy or acceptable candidate to receive God's forgiveness.

Once we genuinely repent, a turning will follow. Instead of disobedience, we choose the path of obedience. Then we can rest in the fact when God sees us He sees *red*, the *Blood of Atonement;* enabling us to walk in the *Spirit of Truth here* and *now,* without the baggage of condemnation.

> …because through Christ Jesus the law of the Spirit of life set me free from the law of sin and death. For what the law was powerless to do in that it was weakened by the sinful nature, God did by sending His Son in the likeness of sinful man, in order that the righteous requirements of the law might be fully met in us, who do not live according to the sinful nature but according to the Spirit.
>
> (Romans 8:2–4 NIV)

It is critically important to become knowledgeable in what the Word says about love and forgiveness. The next step is to walk it out. This will help us understand how to *"lovingly restore"* our brothers and sisters who are making unhealthy and ungodly choices, causing them to waver in their faith and creating havoc in their lives and others.

We are instructed to *"restore gently"* someone who is caught in sin. We must *resist flesh* and *our own opinions.* Regardless of the sin, refuse to be an instrument of doubt and unbelief about our Redeemer's ability and willingness to forgive a truly repentant heart. We too can fall into the same temptations. Godly wisdom is essential! We must never forget sin is sin. Humans measure the severity of sin; not God. He is just and good. Do I understand this, *No* . . . But do I trust Him, *Yes!*

Regardless of how intelligent or how many degrees you may hold, mere humans do not possess the wisdom or love necessary to handle many of the sensitive and painful situations we encounter in this world, but we have a Heavenly Father who does. He will generously pour out His wisdom on all who ask Him. *"If any of you lacks wisdom, he should ask God who gives generously to all without finding fault, and it will be given to him"* (James 1:5 NIV).

Brothers, if someone is caught in a sin, you who are spiritual should *restore him gently*. But watch yourself, or you also may be tempted. Carry each other's burdens, and in this way you will fulfill the law of Christ. If anyone thinks he is something when he is nothing, he deceives himself. Each one should test his own actions. Then he can take pride in himself, without comparing himself to somebody else, for each one should carry his own load.

(Galatians 6:1–5NIV, emphasis added)

Jesus Christ makes the process easy to understand. We are to restore gently, watch ourselves so that we do not fall into temptation, carry each other's burdens, test our own actions, and be careful not to think more highly of ourselves than we ought. To put it simply, *walk in the fear of the Lord!*

As we continue reading scriptures 7–10, we will see and hear a wealth of information when it comes to *"walking out"* a life of love with a Godly character.

Do not be deceived. God cannot be mocked. A man reaps what he sows. The one who sows to please his sinful nature, from that nature will reap destruction; the one who sows to please the Spirit, from the Spirit will reap eternal life. Let us not become weary in doing good, for at the proper time we will reap a harvest if we do not give up. Therefore, as we have opportunity, *let us do good to all people especially to those who belong to the family of Believers.*

(Galatians 6:7–10 NIV, emphasis added)

Daily renewing our minds in Christ will keep our love walk in check. It will bring restoration within our homes, communities, and churches; creating an atmosphere of expectancy for miracles to manifest. This is my prayer and I believe it is an obtainable goal within the Body of Christ!

Because of the destruction and pain caused from bitterness and unforgiveness, I want to focus on *forgiving* in the last portion of this chapter. There is an old saying, *"Unforgiveness is like drinking poison and expecting someone else to die."* When Jesus walked this earth, He left us many beautiful examples of the *power of forgiveness*. If we can grasp this concept and receive the *Truth*, we will see miracles in our lives. Let's begin with a story about a woman with a sinful past. It is too important to leave anything out, so we will read it in its entirety.

Now one of the Pharisees invited Jesus to have dinner with him, so He went to the Pharisee's house and reclined at the table. When a woman who had lived a sinful life in that town learned that Jesus was eating at the Pharisee's house, she brought an alabaster jar of perfume, and as she stood behind Him at His feet weeping, she began to wet His feet with her tears. Then she wiped them with her hair, kissed them and poured perfume on them. When the Pharisee who had invited Him saw this, he said to himself, "If this man were a prophet, He would know who is touching Him and what kind of woman she is, that she is a sinner." Jesus answered him, "Simon, I have something to tell you." "Tell me teacher," he said. "Two men owed money to a certain moneylender. One owed him five hundred denarii's, and the other fifty. Neither of them had the money to pay him back, so he canceled the debts of both. Now which of them will love him more?" Simon replied, "I suppose the one who had the bigger debt canceled." "You have judged correctly," Jesus said. Then He turned toward the woman and said to Simon, "Do you see this woman? I came into your house, you did not give Me any water for My feet, but she wet My feet with her tears and wiped them with her hair. You did not give Me a kiss, but this woman, from the time I entered, has not stopped kissing My feet. You did not put oil on My head, but she has poured perfume on My feet. Therefore, I tell you, her many sins have been forgiven, for she loved much. But he who has been forgiven little loves little." Then Jesus said to her, "Your sins are forgiven." The other guests began to say among them-

selves, "who is this who even forgives sins?" Jesus said
to the woman, "Your faith has saved you; go in peace."
(Luke 7:36–50 NIV)

It was customary in those days and a gesture of hospitality to wash
someone's feet when entering your home. While Jesus reclined, with
His feet extended away from the table, the woman began weeping,
wetting His feet with her tears. Then she wiped the Lord's feet with
her hair. She did for Him what the Pharisee did not. This woman
loved Jesus deeply. Her love for Him was not the basis for her forgiveness. The scriptures tell us she was saved by faith. Her sins were
forgiven and she went away with a peace only God can give. I love
this story, for I too have been forgiven much. It never ceases to amaze
me how merciful and gracious God is to *all* His children.

Next, we will read what happens in our lives after true repentance and forgiveness has been received and embraced.

> After this, Jesus traveled about from one town and village to
> another, proclaiming the good news of the Kingdom of God.
> The twelve were with Him, and also some women who had
> been cured of evil spirits and diseases: Mary (called Magda-
> lene) from whom seven demons had come out; Joanna the
> wife of Cuza, the manager of Herod's household; Susanna
> and many others. *These women were helping to support them
> out of their own means.*
>
> (Luke 8:1–3 NIV, emphasis added)

These women were never the same once Jesus came into their lives.
They embraced His forgiveness and walked in peace. Their faithful service supported Jesus and His disciples in spreading the Good
News to a lost and dying world. No longer living in condemnation
or the shame of their past, they were forgiven!

CHAPTER 15

Test Everything, Hold to Good and Avoid Every Evil

As Christians, we have a responsibility to know and understand God's Word. We are instructed to, *"Study to show thyself approved unto God, a workman that needeth not to be ashamed, rightly dividing the word of Truth"* (2 Timothy 2:15 KJV).

One topic that seems to bring confusion amongst the Body of Christ is *"judging."* Almost everyone knows the scripture *"Judge not, that ye be not judged"* (Matthew 7:1), but do we understand what it means? As Christians, we should not judge self-righteously or hypocritically, however, Christ repeatedly commands us to evaluate a person's character to see if they are genuine. In the New International Version, 1 Thessalonians 5:21, 22 says to, *"Test everything. Hold on to the good. Avoid every kind of evil."* 1 Corinthians 5:9, 2 and Corinthians 11:14, tell us to choose between good and bad.

There is a story in the Bible about a woman caught in adultery and it is an excellent example of the wrong kind of judging. It deals with sin, finger pointing, deceit, and ultimately, *forgiveness.* Anyone knows it takes two participants to commit adultery; however, only the woman stood accused. Provision had been made for the man to escape, using this incident as a stage to trap Jesus. They obviously did not realize who they were dealing with!

> But Jesus went to the Mount of Olives. At dawn He appeared again in the temple courts; where all the people gathered around Him, and He sat down to teach them. The teachers of the law and the Pharisees brought in a woman caught in adultery. They made her stand before the group and said to Jesus, "Teacher this woman was caught

in the act of adultery. In the law Moses commanded us
to stone such women. Now what do you say?

(John 8:1–5 NIV)

The Bible tells us they used this question as a trap because the
Romans did not allow the Jews to carry out death sentences. If Jesus
had said stone her, He could have been in conflict with the Romans.
If Jesus said not to stone her, He could have been accused of being
unsupportive of the law. Stoning was not a prescribed manner of
execution unless the woman was a betrothed virgin. The law also
required the stoning of both parties involved, therefore, the trap was
set.

What Jesus did next was brilliant. He spoke of throwing a stone;
therefore, He could not be accused of failure to uphold the law, yet
the conditions He gave for throwing the stone prevented anyone
from doing so. His wisdom is astounding!

> But Jesus bent down and started to write on the ground
> with His finger. When they kept questioning Him, He
> straightened up and said to them, "If any one of you is
> without sin, let him be the first to throw a stone at her"
> Again, He stooped down and wrote on the ground. At
> this, those who heard began to go away one at a time, the
> older ones first, until only Jesus was left, with the woman
> still standing there. Jesus straightened up and asked her,
> "Woman, where are they? Has no one condemned you?"
> "No one, sir she said." "Then neither do I condemn you,"
> Jesus declared, "Go now and leave your life of sin."
>
> (John 8:6–11 NIV)

Can you imagine what this woman must have been thinking? I have
heard varying opinions about what Jesus wrote on the ground, but I
am particularly partial to the one that suggest He wrote down all the
sins of the accusers. That would certainly shut me up!

This story should make us think twice before eagerly pointing a
self-righteous and hypocritical finger of accusation and judgment.

There is only one person who walked this earth without sin, and His name is Jesus Christ.

Although we are not to hypocritically judge or condemn others, scriptures tell us to test and evaluate a person's fruit and character. It is appropriate to ask questions like: *"Do their words and actions line up? Does their life portray the fruits of the Spirit? Do they bless and edify, or bring confusion and tear down?"* If you are not sure what to look for, Galatians clearly tells us what kind of fruit must be evident in the life of a proclaiming Child of God.

> But the fruit of the Spirit is love, joy, peace, kindness, goodness, faithfulness, gentleness and self-control. Against such things there is no law. Those who belong to Christ Jesus have crucified the sinful nature with its passions and desires. Since we live by the Spirit, let us keep in step with the Spirit. Let us not become conceited, provoking and envying each other.
>
> (Galatians 5:22–26 NIV)

Now that we understand the kind of fruit a Christian should produce, the next step is to prayerfully heed the warning signs and seek *truth*. We live in a world where *truth* is often hard to come by. There are those who walk around in clever disguises but live their lives like a destructive hurricane. They usually leave a path of hurting people they have wounded. Most of the time, it is because they too have been wounded in some way. Regardless of the why, ask the Holy Spirit for discernment and wisdom when dealing with the ferocious wolves that hover about. *They desperately need our prayers, but not necessarily our company!*

> Watch out for false prophets. They come to you in sheep's clothing, but inwardly they are ferocious wolves. *By their fruit you will recognize them.* Do people pick grapes from thorn bushes, or figs from thistle? Likewise every good tree bears good fruit, but a bad tree bears bad fruit, and a good tree cannot bear bad fruit, and a bad tree cannot bear good fruit. Every tree that does not bear good fruit is cut down and

thrown into the fire. Thus, *by their fruit you will recognize them.*
(Matthew 7:13–20 NIV, emphasis added)

We talked in the previous chapter about how to gently restore some-one who is caught in sin, but what do we do when a Believer con-tinues to choose an ungodly path? According to scripture, we have a responsibility to the Lord, the Body of Christ, and ourselves. Sin behavior does not only hurt the person involved, but also destroys and wounds others. This is why the Bible clearly states light has nothing to do with darkness. If we continue to be part of a person's life that chooses to walk in sin, we too can fall into the same tempta-tion. I know this to be a fact from my own personal experience and I do not recommend for anyone to have to learn this lesson the hard way!

We must not grieve the Holy Spirit. We cannot make someone do right, but we can love and encourage him or her to turn away from sin so that blessings can be restored to their life. The follow-ing scriptures offer great insights on what is expected from us when dealing with these issues. It is a hard word, but it must be adhered to if we expect God's blessings.

If we truly put into practice these instructions, a hypocrite would not last long in our churches. In fact, we would have a sold out Body of Believers winning the lost and performing miracles in the name of Jesus.

> I have written you in my letters not to associate with sexually immoral people, not at all meaning the people of this world who are immoral, or the greedy and swindlers, or idolaters, in that case leave this world. But now I am writing you that you must not associate with anyone who calls himself a brother but is sexually immoral, or greedy, an idolater or a slanderer, a drunkard or a swindler. With such a man do not eat. What business is it of mine to judge those outside the church? *Are you not to judge those inside? God will judge those outside.* Expel the wicked man from among you.
> (1 Corinthians 5:9–13 NIV, emphasis added)

Paul was not instructing the church to disassociate from the world of sinners. In fact, he says if we did, we would have to *"leave this world."* On the contrary, he is instructing the Believers not to associate with *those who say they are Christians yet live like the world.* To be blunt, their fruit stinks and their words do not line up with their actions. He says, *"With such a man do not even eat!"*

Total perfection will not be achieved on this earth; we all fall short, however, we should be striving for holiness, not trying to find ways to sin. Keep in mind, the difference between a hypocrite and a genuine Christian is this: The truly repentant heart will make a change and cease from walking down a sinful and destructive path.

There is another responsibility we have as God's children, and that is To *keep our tongue from evil!* This is not the time to call up a friend and share the bad news that someone has blown it. Gossip is hurtful and can hinder or delay an individual from getting right with God. We must pray and intercede, not gossip and tear down.

> If anyone has caused grief, he has not so much grieved me as he has grieved all of you, to some extent, not to put it too severely. The punishment inflicted on him by the majority is sufficient for him. Now instead, you ought to forgive and comfort him, so that he will not be overwhelmed by excessive sorrow. I urge you, therefore, to reaffirm your love for him.
> (2 Corinthians 2:5–8 NIV)

In these scriptures Paul is speaking about a particular person who was caught in a serious offense in Corinth. Church discipline had been imposed and this individual displayed true repentance. Paul urges the Corinthians to *"forgive and comfort him, so that he will not be overwhelmed by excessive sorrow . . . reaffirm your love for him."*

Even though discipline is painful and difficult, God's love remains constant. His Word says He loves those He chastises. If we choose to humble ourselves during times of discipline, the result will be a strong and growing relationship with the Father.

Endure hardship as discipline; God is treating you as sons.
For what son is not disciplined by his father? If you are
not disciplined (and everyone undergoes discipline), then
you are illegitimate children and not true sons. Moreover,
we have all had human fathers who disciplined us and we
respected them for it. How much more should we submit to
the Father of our spirits and live! Our fathers disciplined us
for a little while as they thought best; but God disciplines
us for our good, that we may share in His holiness. No discipline seems pleasant at the time, but painful. Later on,
however, it produces a harvest of righteousness and peace
for those who have been trained by it. Therefore, *strengthen
your feeble arms and weak knees. Make level paths for your
feet, so that the lame may not be disabled, but rather healed.*
(Hebrews 12:5–13 NIV, emphasis added)

God does not contradict Himself, change His mind, add to or take
away from His Word. His promises are *Yes* and *Amen!* To live a life
pleasing to the Father we must *"strengthen our feeble arms and weak
knees, and make level paths for our feet."* Why? So that the lame will
walk, the blind will see, and the lost will find Jesus. To accomplish
this awesome task we will endure discipline, but the outcome produces a *"harvest of righteousness and peace!"*

Never lose sight of the fact God is constantly at work in our lives
to fulfill His plans and divine purposes. Walking that path means we
will endure discipline, but it is all for our good. Just as a child grows
and matures, our spiritual lives should reflect growth and maturity.

All scripture is God breathed and is useful for teaching,
rebuking, correcting and training in righteousness, *so that
the man of God may be thoroughly equipped for every good work.*
(2 Timothy 3:16, 17 NIV, emphasis added)

How can the Body of Christ achieve a healthy balance that will
produce lasting Kingdom fruit? I believe these few simple steps will

prepare the way: Ask God for an understanding of scripture, be willing to apply what we learn, seek wisdom to discern fruit, and choose to bear one another's burdens with love and compassion. While there is still time, we must work together in unity and love.

> In the presence of God and of Christ Jesus, who will judge the living and the dead, and in view of His appearing and His kingdom, I give you this charge: *Preach the Word; be prepared in season and out of season; correct, rebuke, and encourage, with great patience and careful instruction.*
> (2 Timothy 4:1, 2 NIV, emphasis added)

> Finally, brothers, *whatever is true, whatever is noble, whatever is right, whatever is pure, whatever is lovely; whatever is admirable—if anything is excellent or praiseworthy—think about such things.* Whatever you have learned or received or heard from me, or seen in me *put it into practice,* and the God of peace will be with you.
> (Philippians 4:8, 9 NIV, emphasis added)

Although my life made a dramatic and positive change, it was not until I endured some much-needed discipline. Through it all, I came to understand how precious a *"bountiful harvest of righteousness and peace"* could be.

CHAPTER 16

Beauty for Ashes, Joy for Mourning

Have you ever been driving along and *bang,* you hear a crash and feel pain? Suddenly your brain says, *"Hey, I've just been in a car accident."* It's a funny thing how the sound of medal bending and airbags going off in your face can make a lasting impression. Physically, I seemed to be in one piece, but my little Daytona was totaled. Then I remembered, *"Man, I just paid this car off and got a brand new paint job, now this."* The saying is true, *"Some days are better spent in bed!"*

The other driver involved did not suffer any injuries and received a lot less damage to his vehicle. I felt pain down my back and neck, with visible burns and bruises caused by the airbag and seatbelt, but looking at my car made me thankful I had my seatbelt on.

Paramedics hovered about insisting I go to the emergency room, reassuring me it was in my best interest. Feeling a little unsteady and banged up, I agreed to go.

On the way to the hospital I felt a small lump about the size of a pea protruding from the left side of my neck. The paramedics saw it too but figured the impact of the airbag and crash caused it. The doctor in the emergency room decided to take additional x-rays, just to be on the safe side. Everything checked out fine except for a few bruises, burns, and pulled muscles. According to the doctor, the lump had nothing to do with the accident and he insisted I make an appointment for further test. I said okay, anxious to get home and cry on Daddy's shoulder!

Just in case you are interested, the accident was my fault. Cars stopped for me to cross through an intersection but they failed to notice someone approaching in the far left hand lane. Actually, a man in a van saw the on-coming car but thought I could make it across, so he continued to motion for me to go and I happily forged ahead. *You should never do this . . . Take my word for it!*

Approximately a month later the lump had grown a little and bothered me when I wore a turtleneck top or any kind of collar. I decided to make an appointment and get it checked. The doctor stated it appeared to be a soft tissue growth, not commonly associated with a malignant type tumor. He scheduled out patient surgery to remove it. No big deal, right?

Several days later the doctor left an urgent message on my answering machine. He insisted I call him ASAP to discuss the tumor . . . *Tumor!* When did the pea size lump turn into a tumor?

I didn't know what to do. It had been a little over a year since Mom passed away with lymphoma cancer and dealing with the loss had been difficult for everyone. My poor father still walked around in a daze, and *what about Bob!* You see, something amazing had happened shortly after my car accident; he came back into my life.

When mother passed away, Bob came to her funeral and that was the first time in years I had seen him, but we did not even speak to each other. Some time later, I was washing my car in the driveway and he drove by and decided to stop and talk. We began briefly catching up on one another's lives. Bob shared with me how his marriage of fifteen years had fallen apart, but how grateful he was for the beautiful daughter God blessed them with. She was an answer to his prayers. Her name is Traci and interestingly enough we share the same birthday, February 6.

As we discussed problems we both experienced in our marriages my heart raced and thoughts whirled around my head, *"Good heavens, it's been almost seventeen years. Does Bob realize I never stopped loving him?"* At that moment, I decided to tell him how I felt and let the chips fall where they may. I blurted out, *"Bob, I need you to know something, I still love you and I probably always will."* We both just looked at each other as tears ran down our faces. Then our conversation turned to the past. We discussed the self-destructive mess my life became after the hysterectomy, and how everything changed when they properly diagnosed the disease I suffered with for so many years. The more we talked I realized how much I had missed my friend, and how good it felt to be with him once again.

Facing Dad and Bob about this new health crisis would not be easy, so I made a plan not say anything until I knew the facts. My appointment was the following day, so I waited . . . *and I prayed!* The day of the appointment, I nervously walked into the doctor's office to discuss the "tumor." His countenance said it all. He started off with, *"I'm sorry but . . ."* I knew immediately the report was not good. Then he said something my brain refused to accept. *"The results came back as a malignant soft tissue sarcoma in the third stages of cancer. The cancer is very rare and it's imperative to see a specialist immediately. I am sorry to have to give you this news, but please keep in touch and let me know how things turn out. I wish you well."* When he finished talking I started laughing, and said, *"Okay, thanks, doc."* Knowing my medical history my response concerned him. I reassuringly said, *"I've cried enough over the years about my health, I might as well try something new."* Then I left his office and headed to my car.

Before I knew it reality hit. Pulling over on the side of the road I tried to collect my thoughts. *"Rare cancer, stage three, I wish you well. What . . . How can this be? I spent my whole life suffering with a blood disease, surviving insurmountable odds, including death! This cannot be happening. I'm finally enjoying life without the constant dread of pain and hospitals. On top of everything else, I have to go home and tell Dad."*

Arriving home, I sat in the driveway and prayed this prayer: *"God give me the strength to tell Dad. He depends on me so much since Mama went to be with You. He needs me, and oh yeah, Please Father, don't let me die! I'm just starting to enjoy life. Remember the angel You sent to my bedside when I lay dying in the hospital. It said, and I quote, 'Many children will pass through your arms and be blessed, there is still a work for you to do. You will not leave this earth until your work is complete.' God, I've made a lot of mistakes, but I haven't held those children yet or completed the work You sent me to do. Please, don't let me have lived through all that just to end up dying from cancer! So here's the deal, I refuse to depend on a doctor to determine the outcome of my life. I'm in Your hands. Forgive me for the times I have disappointed You, and please tell Mama I love her but it will be a while before I see her again. I love you Jesus . . . Amen!"*

After saying that prayer I thought about Bob, and how after all these years we had a second chance at love. How in the world was I going to tell him I had cancer! My thoughts changed drastically and I prayed once again. *"Okay God, is this a joke? Why would you allow Bob back in my life when I am once again facing a serious illness and possibly death? I broke up with him years ago because of sickness. Is it fair to put him through this again? By the way, why is it every time we have an opportunity to be together my life bites? Sorry God, but I might as well say it; You already know what I'm thinking. Forgive me, but I'd really like to know the answer to this one!"*

Thunder and lightning did not come out of the sky and zap me, so I figured things were okay between God and me. Although I did not have any answers, I still loved Bob deeply. My first priority would be to tell Dad and then I would talk to Bob.

Taking a deep breath, I gathered my thoughts, got out of the car and went inside. Dad was lying down but not asleep, so I sat on the bed and told him the news. He looked away in shock and disbelief. I tried to be positive and upbeat, reminding him what my guardian angel promised years earlier; however, I don't think he heard anything after the dreaded word, *cancer*.

Next thing on my list . . . telling Bob. Not wanting to repeat the same mistakes I made seventeen years earlier, I decided not to push him away this time. I would let him choose to stay or go. He chose well, and stayed! Bob remained true to his nature and rock solid. He said he was not going anywhere and we would get through this together.

The next day I awoke focused and determined to beat this thing. Dad wanted me to call Mom's cancer specialist. He was a good doctor and we trusted him. I called his office and he rearranged his schedule to see us that afternoon. Looking over the surgeon's report he appeared stunned and confused. Our family had been through so much in the past year and he could not believe what he was reading. After processing his thoughts he arranged for us to go directly to the office of an Ear Nose and Throat Specialist. We tearfully hugged goodbye and thanked him.

The Specialist wasted no time, stating I definitely had a very rare soft tissue sarcoma in the third stages of cancer. He wanted to do some research and meet with a few colleagues before proceeding with any kind of treatment.

Within a few days, we were back in his office. He began with, *"There are very few documented cases of this type of cancer and it does not respond to chemotherapy. Radical surgery will be necessary to remove the tumor, surrounding muscles, and anything I feel may possibly be affected. It is a reoccurring cancer and there are no guarantees. Case reports show surgery with radiation are our only options and may prolong a reoccurrence, but I cannot say how soon before another one. The surgery is our first priority and will most likely leave you somewhat disfigured with extensive scarring."* We thanked him, scheduled surgery and left.

Driving home, I reminded Dad of everything I'd overcome and how God had always come through. I tried to encourage him by saying, *"Don't worry Daddy; this will be a piece of cake."* He smiled, but was not buying my optimism.

I knew I needed the Lord's help in a big way but how do you ask God for healing with the shame of divorce and a life full of mistakes and bad choices hanging over your head? Bob and I both suffered with so much shame and condemnation; we had not grasped the concept of God's forgiveness. Feeling unworthy to ask for help or a miracle, somehow we found the courage to go for it anyway. *So often that is all God is waiting for, a truly repentant heart willing to ask Him for help in spite of their mess or shortcomings.*

Although Bob and I talked for hours on the phone and saw each other as often as possible, we had not officially started dating. Due to our history and recent divorces, we felt awkward being seen together. We knew the rumor mill and wagging tongues would jump into high gear, and we were not looking forward to going through that. With my surgery right around the corner, we decided to wait until it was over and I had recuperated to go out on a real date.

The day of surgery arrived. Doctors removed everything they felt the tumor might have affected, including several muscles and nerves.

Even though the procedure was quite extensive and half my neck and chest had been cut open, I did not have the disfiguration they prepared us for, just heavy scarring. Radiation therapy was recommended to delay a rapid developing reoccurrence but I decided to place total trust in God, refusing any further treatment. Dad stayed prayerfully by my side, but after losing Mother I knew he could not take any additional stress, therefore, I kept this decision quiet. For the first time in my entire life, I wanted to have the final say about what anyone did to my body!

My refusal for treatment did not go unchallenged. The doctor strongly disagreed. I tried to explain that after researching the effects of radiation, it appeared that without a spleen and a sufficient immune system, the side affects caused from the treatment could be devastating. He could not refute my claim, so my decision stood firm.

Everyday I asked God to look past my faults and heal me. Little did I know His plans were so much bigger than I dared to dream or imagine. He knew something important; the little girl who grew up trusting Him with her whole heart would soon come out of hiding. She was finally on the path to learning how to *fall* into a *life changing trust relationship* with Him. You see, in spite of all my failures the Father still had a *good plan* for my future.

The majority of my life had been spent dependent on doctors and medicine, only to end up in worse shape with lots of ugly scars. Although I did not know what to do, I continued to pray and God filled me with an unexplainable peace, surrounding me like a blanket of love and protection. My plans were quite simple: Trust God (even though I knew I did not deserve His mercy), stay positive and happy, and hold on tight to Bob.

After a few days of recuperating, Bob and I went on our first official date. A huge bandage adorned my neck like an ugly necklace, but I felt blessed and excited to be alive. Many obstacles lay ahead but we planned to face them together.

The next year proved to be quite an adventure. When they removed the bandages from around my neck, I looked like the "Bride of Frankenstein." As the months progressed and to the doctors amazement, I continued to show no reoccurring signs of cancer, but he took every opportunity to remind me of the statistics and voice his disapproval over my decision to decline further treatment. Although every documented case showed a rapid reoccurrence, God remained faithfully and mysteriously at work.

During that year, our family dealt with a number of challenges and changes. Dad suffered another stroke, heart attack, and two triple by-pass surgeries. God's mercy prevailed and Dad made a full recovery. When he got well, some friends played matchmaker and set him up with Polly, an old acquaintance from Mississippi. Both widowed and in need of companionship, they began dating. Before long, they were married and embarking on a new life together. Their marriage gave Bob and I time to focus on each other and develop a stronger, more mature relationship.

One huge obstacle for us had to do with the past, and the fact I ran to Dad for everything. Bob knew this and needed assurance I had grown up in this areas of my life. Determined not to lose him again, I prayed for God to show me what to do, *and He did.*

The first time we met Bob pursued me, now the roles were reversed. With unashamed determination, I set out on a mission to prove my complete trust and devotion to him. I honestly think he enjoyed this turn of events. Being pursued can be fun when it is someone you are passionately in love with!

I want to close this chapter with a message for those who are facing cancer. I understand what a difficult time this is. Your doctors may have recommended chemotherapy or radiation. It is your life and only you can make that decision! Seek God for wisdom and do your own research. A doctor's job is to present the facts and determine the best possible treatment. You have the final say. Whatever you choose, God is able and willing to carry you through to victory.

Do not allow the facts to destroy your faith in God's power and ability to do the impossible. He promises to never leave or forsake us and His Word also says, *"The Lord will fulfill His purpose for me"* (Psalm 138:8 NIV).

Grab hold of His promises and with a bulldog mentality take a bite, hold on, and do not let go, no matter how long it takes. God is the Great Physician and He is an on time God. His promises *are for you* and they are *Yes* and *Amen.* Your very life depends on your decision to *believe, receive,* and *stand* on this *Truth!*

> For no matter how many promises God has made, they are *"Yes"* in Christ. And so through Him the *"Amen"* is spoken by us to the glory of God. Now it is God who makes both us and you stand firm in Christ. He anointed us, set His seal of ownership on us, and put His Spirit in our hearts as a deposit, guaranteeing what is to come.
>
> (2 Corinthians 1:20–22 NIV, emphasis added)

God used cancer to teach Bob and I the importance of getting His Word inside our heart and speaking it forth with our mouth. His glory was revealed in ways we never dreamed possible. As our faith continued to grow and a few years later, you will see how the Lord opened doors for my healing testimony to be shared to other nations around the world; *spreading the Good News of this wonderful Father, Savior, Redeemer, Healer, and Friend!*

CHAPTER 17

Learning What It Means To Be Forgiven

From the moment we began *"officially dating"* I asked Bob to marry me. This is not exactly proper etiquette, but wasting time was not on my agenda! It is not every day a second chance like this comes along. Some things are just meant to be.

We did not feel comfortable getting married in our hometown. Wearing the *"divorce"* label created quite a little scandal in our church community, especially with our history together. A select few envisioned us going around in sackcloth and ashes for the rest of our lives. Some even felt cancer was God's punishment for divorce, and the thought of asking Him to heal me seemed quite brazen and beyond their comprehension!

It is a terrible thing to go through life with such an angry image of God. He is not a tyrant waiting to slap us into hell every time we mess up. The only way to get a glimpse of His loving character is to spend time in the Word and walk in a committed relationship with Him. I can spend hours talking about God's love, goodness, and compassion, but each person has to experience and receive their own revelation of His all-consuming unexplainable love. Once it happens, you are never the same!

Feeling a little wild and crazy and wanting to get out from under the microscope, we made plans to fly to Las Vegas and elope. Dad and Polly were happy and gave us their blessing. Polly and I went shopping and she bought me a beautiful wedding dress. It was simple yet elegant and made me feel like a princess.

The morning we boarded the plane Bob finally officially proposed. I suppose he wanted to make it legit! When I see television shows with romantic and extravagant proposals I sometimes wish I had practiced a little more self-control, but playing hard to get was a game I could not afford to risk. Years earlier, I put Bob through schizophrenic torture, and he needed constant reassurance I was focused, steady, and serious.

Bob made all the arrangements and did an outstanding job! In true *"fairy tale"* fashion, a limousine picked us up and whisked us off to "The Little Chapel of Flowers." Just in case you are wondering, Elvis did not perform the ceremony; however, we did have some comical moments. Our driver had a heavy New York accent and proved to be very multi-talented. He took our wedding photos, stood up as our witness, and escorted us all over Vegas in the limo.

After the ceremony, we headed back to the hotel. Before proceeding with our honeymoon plans, we felt compelled to pray together as man and wife. Kneeling down by the bed we repented of our past, giving our future and lives completely over to God. We gave Him permission to do whatever He wanted with us. As the burden of sin and condemnation lifted, our hearts exploded with joy and uncontrollable weeping.

Something new and beautiful began at that very moment, its called forgiveness! Feeling deep humility and gratefulness to God, we did not know what the future held but planned on living life to the fullest. We made a decision not to dwell on cancer or thoughts of death and to keep each other encouraged. I do not believe I have ever felt as alive as I did that day. Forgiveness is truly one of God's greatest medicines.

When the blood of Jesus is applied to sin, an amazing and miraculous transformation happens. You can physically feel the burden and weight of sin lift. Our sins are not only forgiven but they are thrown into *"the depths of the sea"* never to be held against us again!

> You will again have compassion on us; You will tread our sins underfoot and hurl all our iniquities into the depths of the sea.
>
> (Micah 7:19 NIV)

An overcoming and blessed future depended on our willingness to receive this awesome gift of forgiveness. Yes, there are consequences for our choices; however, we did not want to be held prisoners to the past. Choosing to embrace this gift meant we were free from the burden of condemnation and guilt. We could walk in the anticipation and excitement of God's blessings, His liberty, and freedom.

It took a while to overcome the past with it's shame and condemnation and become bold about our newfound happiness. The process was not immediate. There were times when a certain few wanted to dredge up the past and we had to learn to remind ourselves of the forgiveness Jesus lovingly extended toward us when we repented. In time, I became outspoken enough to tell those who liked to remind me of my many sins, *"I have given that to God and He forgave me. When I bring up a past sin, He simply responds, 'Donna, what sin?'* Then I would end the conversation with, *"In the future, please take your concerns to God. He is the one with all the answers. I am just the one He forgave."* This response pretty much nipped things in the bud!

For any of you who are struggling in this area, let me share an illustration that might be helpful. If a couple engages in premarital sex they can ask God to forgive them, and He will. That sin will be thrown into *"the depths of the sea"* and never be held against them again; however, what if they become pregnant? Is God punishing them? No! We reap what we sow and this is simply a consequence of sex. When the baby arrives in nine months, they have a choice: Embrace God's forgiveness and raise their child in the joy and fear of the Lord, or live in shame and see this precious life as punishment instead of blessing!

This child can be a reminder of God's forgiveness as they teach by example how to enjoy and appreciate a loving relationship with their Creator. When the child grows up and makes his or her own mistakes, they will remember the example set before them by their parents. Instead of living in bondage and shame, they can walk in freedom with a heart's desire to serve God in gratitude and praise. This is something all parents should want for their children.

When Bob and I knelt down and prayed that day in the motel room our hearts felt heavy with shame, but we rose to our feet forgiven and full of hope. We longed to get on with our life without the weight of condemnation, and that is exactly what we did. It was a wonderful way to start a life together. Next on the agenda . . . Sightseeing!

Anxious to get out of the *big* city of Vegas, we rented a car and set out on the highway to explore the countryside. Our first stop, the Hoover Dam and then off to the Grand Canyon, yet nothing prepared us for its beauty. Everyone should see it at least once in his or her lifetime. The world is full of magnificent portraits God has painted for us to enjoy, as a reminder of how *Great* and *Powerful* He truly is!

Heading home, we felt anxious and excited about the future. Little did we know the cleansing, purging, pruning, and molding that lay ahead. Entering this covenant with our Redeemer meant our lives belonged entirely to Him. Going through the motions of being a Christian and serving God was no longer an option. The time had come to grow up, get serious, and learn how to die to the things of flesh, which destroy and bring pain. Just as Paul wrote, flesh has to die so that Christ may be exalted and live.

> For to me, to live is Christ and to die is gain.
>
> (Philippians 1:22 NIV)

There is a reason the Bible refers to our Christian walk as a *"narrow road."* The path is not easy, causing many to give up and quit before even getting started. It is a humbling experience filled with growing pains. We often question, *"What will it cost? What do I have to give up? Will I really be happy? Is it worth it?"* We must decide for ourselves, no one can do it for us.

Sometimes our attempts to serve God have ulterior motives, such as pleasing others or the fear of going to hell, and we are left wondering why we lack fulfillment and feel like a failure. Only when we fall in love with Jesus Christ and get sick and tired of complacency, mediocrities, and limited blessings, can we realize the wonderful benefits of walking the *"straight and narrow,"* with pleasing the Father as our only motive. The question is, *"Will flesh or Spirit rule our lives?"*

God does not make *bad* things; therefore, flesh is not bad; however, when we allow it to dictate our thoughts and actions the results can be dangerous and destructive. This is why the subject of flesh vs. Spirit is so important.

Let's look at an example. Flesh would like to eat ice cream or chocolate everyday, watch television, avoid work, and play nonstop. This is not God's best, and because of the law of sowing and reaping, it will yield a troublesome harvest of obesity, health problems, relationship issues, depression, loneliness, and the list goes on and on. If we will strive to obey God, the benefits will be great, and out of our lives will flow blessings for ourselves, and others. The bottom line is this, when we strive to satisfy flesh with no self-control or balance toward the things of God, we will reap a harvest of pain and suffering.

When we choose to walk with Christ, dying to flesh is no easy task. We need the help of the Holy Spirit and the Word of God actively inside our hearts. It is important to learn how to encourage ourselves in the Lord, just as King David learned to do. Above all, do not despair or allow yourself to take the easy way out by doing just enough to get by. Anyone who has fallen into this trap knows how miserable life can become.

As you continue to cast down and deny flesh, your spirit man grows stronger and more dominant. The key is to submit to God and resist the devil, by doing this you will be greatly rewarded for your obedience.

> Submit yourselves, then, to God. Resist the devil, and he will flee from you. Come near to God, and He will come near to you.
>
> (James 4:7, 8 NIV)

When someone says I love you, there is an expectation, and rightfully so. You anticipate spending time with that person and being a priority in their life. If this does not happen, you begin doubting their words. In fact, insecurities and feelings of hurt will surface, causing you to wonder if they truly ever loved you. If the issues are not resolved, it will destroy the relationship. Many times the root of the problem is a destructive selfish spirit.

For many years, this is how I treated God. In desperate and lonely moments I cried out to Him for help. Mercifully, He came to my rescue as He patiently waited to have a genuine and intimate relationship with me. Somewhere along the way I had lost my *"First Love"* and no longer knew what pleased the heart of God. It breaks my heart to admit it, but I did not know because I did not care enough to find out. Finally facing the ugly truth was the first step to repentance and beginning a new and exciting *"love walk"* with the Lord.

God is a loving, patient, and jealous Father who longs for His children to desire intimacy with Him. When we are passionate about something, nothing can stop our pursuit. He saw ahead and knew one day I would go after Him with the same zeal and determination I used to pursue Bob. Just the thought of this must have pleased His heart tremendously. Never have I had a friend as loving and faithful as He. For the first time in many years, my words and actions line up. I can say with sincerity, *"Jesus, I love and appreciate You. With every breath I take I desire nothing more than to please You!"*

Now is a good time to take a moment and examine your own life. Too often, our lips say we love the Lord and want to serve Him, but our actions reveal the *truth*. Allow the Holy Spirit to speak to your heart. Ask Him to show you how to draw near to God and the path to a loving and healthy relationship with the Father.

Jesus Christ is the only reason I am alive and breathing today. I am a living example that no life is too messed up; instead, it is an awesome opportunity for God to show His power and might, so that He may receive the glory and the honor.

Right now as you read these words, express your love and gratitude for His undying grace and mercy. Refuse to allow your circumstances to dictate or define your relationship with the Father. Rejoice in Him and keep a thankful heart of praise. This will swing open wide the door to miracles in your life.

Today can be a brand-new beginning. Come before the Lord with a repentant heart and desire to please the Father. Once you have done this, let go of the past and begin anew. With determination and zeal, draw near to God and be assured He will draw near to you. The things of this world are temporary but the things of God are eternal. Seek Him today and don't delay!

> Forget the former things; do not dwell on the past. See, I am doing a new thing! Now it springs up; do you not perceive it? I am making a way in the desert and streams in the wasteland.
>
> (Isaiah 43:18, 19 NIV)

Take the time to open your Bible to Deuteronomy, chapter twenty-eight. Read both the blessings and the curses. It should give you a greater desire to walk in obedience reaping the benefits of God's blessings.

Keep in mind that He is *not* a God of favoritism. What He has done for me He will do for you, but you must choose to *believe, receive, and expect!* Make the scriptures personal by writing your name in them. Once you have done this speak them out in faith and walk it out with your life. In grateful anticipation expect a miracle.

> The Lord will open the heavens, the storehouse of His bounty, to send rain on your land in season and to bless all the work of your hands. You will lend to many nations but will borrow from none. The Lord will make you the head, not the tail, if you pay attention to the commands of the Lord your God that I give you this day and carefully follow them, you will always be at the top, never at the bottom.
>
> (Deuteronomy 28:12, 13 NIV)

> Yet the Lord longs to be gracious to you; He rises to show you compassion. For the Lord is a God of justice. Blessed are all who wait for Him.
>
> (Isaiah 30:18 NIV)

And I pray, that you being rooted and established in love, may have power, together with all the saints, to grasp how wide and long and high and deep is the love of Christ, and to know this love that surpasses knowledge, that you may be filled to the measure of all the fullness of God. *Now to Him who is able to do immeasurably more than all we ask or imagine, according to His power that is at work within us,* to Him be glory in the church and in Christ Jesus through-out all generations, forever and ever! Amen."

(Ephesians 3:17–21 NIV, emphasis added)

Our journey of *falling* into a growing trust relationship with God was just beginning, and more miracles were right around the corner!

CHAPTER 18

Marriage According to God

There are many books on marriage telling us *how to* or *how not to*, but the best book you will ever read is the Bible. If both parties will walk according to the Word of God, your home will be filled with His blessings, peace, and joy, even if you have an extended family. In today's society there are many blended combinations, but God's Word will work in every home when applied in love and wisdom.

I am not suggesting you will never have struggles. Let me be perfectly clear, *you will!* The good news is we have a Father who hears and answers prayer. We also have the Holy Spirit to instruct and guide us in the wisdom needed to bring harmony and peace within our relationships and family structure.

Wise instructions for daily living can be found in 1 Peter, chapter three. It encourages us to do what is right, even when it hurts …Ouch! Be compassionate, never repay evil for evil, and live in harmony.

> For, whoever would love life and see good days must keep his tongue from evil and his lips from deceitful speech. He must turn from evil and do good; He must seek peace and pursue it. For the eyes of the Lord are on the righteous and His ears are attentive to their prayer, but the face of the Lord is against those who do evil. Who is going to harm you if you are eager to do good? But even if you should suffer for what is right, you are blessed. Do not fear what they fear; do not be frightened, but in your hearts set apart Christ as Lord. Always be prepared to give an answer to everyone who asks you to give a reason for the hope that you have. But

> do this with a gentleness and respect, keeping a clear con-
> science, so that those who speak maliciously against your
> good behavior in Christ may be ashamed of their slander.
> It is better, if it is God's will, to suffer for doing good than
> for doing evil. For Christ died for sins once for all, the righ-
> teous for the unrighteous, to bring you to God.
>
> (1 Peter 3:10–18 NIV)

If we put these scriptures into practice, our relationships will not be torn apart due to a lack of respect for one another and selfish choices. A Christian's home should be an example to the world. Couples should be particularly careful not to belittle, ridicule, and disrespect one another (or their children) in public or private. We must choose to behave like men and women of God. This world is in desperate need of Christian examples who actively demonstrate love and respect toward each other. I grew up hearing, *"Your life is the only Bible some people read"* and guess what, it's true! By living this way, people will want what we have instead of running the other direc-tion trying to avoid us.

When faced with difficult family situations, it is always best to pray before reacting. The Holy Spirit will give us wisdom but we have a responsibility to take that knowledge and put it to work in a loving way. The Lord will not do it for us.

Doing the right thing is not always the easiest or most popular, but for a Christian it is the *only* way. When we choose to disregard and not uphold the Word of God in our homes, we open the door to confusion, pain, and chaos.

> Live in peace with each other. And we urge you, broth-
> ers, warn those who are idle, encourage the timid, help the
> weak, be patient with everyone. Make sure that nobody
> pays back wrong for wrong, but always try to be kind to
> each other and to everyone else. Be joyful always, pray con-
> tinually; give thanks in all circumstances, for this is God's
> will for you in Christ Jesus.
>
> (1 Thessalonians 5:13–18 NIV)

Bob and I longed for a healthy and God-centered marriage. Together we promised to do right and strive to live in peace with everyone. Extended family issues and critical spirits did not always make this an easy task. There were those who did not understand how we could get on with our lives as though divorce never happened. We were painfully aware of the negative effects of a broken home, however, staying in a pit of guilt and condemnation only keeps you beat down, and prevents you from being fruitful. According to scripture, this is not God's will and purpose. Once He has forgiven you, get up and get on with your life. Remember to keep your tongue from evil, walk in love toward others, pray for those who persecute you, refuse to allow bitterness in your heart, and *leave the results to God!*

You cannot talk about marriage without discussing the subject of money. Some people feel an overwhelming desire to control the finances in their home as a symbol of power. I have two words for you, *stop it!* This is not scriptural and a Christian should not display such behavior.

We must also be careful not to make money an idol. In 1 Timothy 6:10 we are told, *"The love of money is a root of all kinds of evil."* Some people confuse this scripture and quote it incorrectly stating, *"Money is the root of all kinds of evil."* The Bible clearly says it is the *"love of money."*

According to statistics, the almighty dollar is one of the main reasons marriages end in divorce. Christian homes were not exempt from this study. In fact, the final analysis showed just as many Christian marriages were broken and destroyed due to money issues. This is a sad testimony and it hinders the world from seeing how abundantly God will bless His people when they walk in total obedience. For this very reason, financial problems are not only dangerous, but also foolish! As Christians, we must pray for wisdom when dealing with money matters. Couples should work together and create a system that will meet their needs and bring harmony and unity, not division and animosity.

What about the issue of tithing, is it something we have to do? This is a subject very close to my heart because I know first hand how beautifully it works, and there are too many Christian families needlessly struggling with money issues. My desire is for everyone to enjoy God's blessings, not just a few.

He promises in Malachi to *"rebuke the devour and pour out such a blessing on us we will not have room enough to contain it."* We must not rob God of His portion in order to receive these blessings. God instructs us to be good stewards of all He has blessed us with, and having an *"it's my money"* mentality is an attitude we cannot afford to walk in.

> Will a man rob God? Yet you rob Me. But you ask, how do we rob You? In tithes and offerings. You are under a curse, the whole nation of you, because you are robbing Me. Bring the whole tithe into the storehouse, that there may be food in My house. *Test Me in this, says the Lord Almighty, and see if I will not throw open the floodgates of heaven and pour out so much blessing that you will not have room enough for it.* I will prevent pest from devouring your crops, and the vines in your field will not casts their fruit, says the Lord Almighty.
>
> (Malachi 3:8–11 NIV, emphasis added)

Some argue tithing was abolished with the law, the Old Testament. I have heard people claim it is not even mentioned in the New Testament. Let's look in Matthew chapter 23 and see what Jesus has to say about the matter.

In this chapter, He is issuing a strong rebuke. Jesus is not criticizing the observance of the law but He opposes the hypocrisy involved, stating; *"You should have practiced the latter, without neglecting the former."* They were doing right by giving the tenth, but like any seasoned hypocrite, they neglected the more important matters.

> Woe to you, teachers of the law and Pharisees, you hypocrites! You give a tenth of your spices, mint, dill, and cumin. But you have neglected the more important matters of the law, justice, mercy, and faithfulness. *You should have practiced the latter, without neglecting the former.*
>
> (Matthew 23:23 NIV, emphasis added)

God can do amazing things with a budget when we walk in obedience. It does not matter if it is one hundred or one thousand dollars a week, if you will tithe and give generously, God will miraculously protect your finances and meet your needs.

> I am young and now I am old, yet I have never seen the righteous forsaken or their children begging bread. They are always generous and lend freely; their children will be blessed.
>
> (Psalm 37:25, 26 NIV)

Scripture also tells us to be cheerful givers. We should not have a *"brat"* attitude. Growing up in the church I heard people say some crazy things, such as, *"I've paid tithes for years and God better come through for me"* or *"I paid tithes this week so that God will bless me with . . ."* You can fill in the blank. We have an *"I'll scratch your back you scratch mine"* mentality. How foolish and selfish we must look to the Father when we act like a spoiled demanding child. If our hearts are right toward the things of God, our attitudes will reflect a life of praise and cheerful giving. We cannot pick or choose what we want to be obedient about; we are to obey the Word in every area of our lives, *including finances!*

If there is a problem with money in your marriage, talk to your spouse. Spend time in prayer and fasting (yes fasting), and ask the Holy Spirit for wisdom. Be obedient, His Word will not fail! *"Test Me in this, says the Lord Almighty . . ."*

If you are married and your spouse is not a Christian, explain the importance of faithfulness in committing to God what is His. Be prepared, have scripture ready and a *gentle spirit!* Ask the Holy Spirit to help you choose your words wisely. *Do not* argue, accuse, or raise your voice. Keep the following scriptures in mind and although it says *"wives,"* when applied it works for men as well. Over the years, I have heard many testimonies of men and women coming to the Lord because of their spouse's behavior and loving spirit.

> Wives, in the same way be submissive to your husbands so that, if any of them do not believe the Word, they may be won over without words by the behavior of their wives, when they see the purity and reverence of your lives.
>
> (1 Peter 3:1, 2 NIV)

If you are single, begin today committing your finances to God. When seeking a mate, make sure they understand your convictions and study the scriptures together. *This matter should be settled before entering the covenant of marriage.*

CHAPTER 19

A Matter of Trust

God's plans for Bob and I involved healing, restoration, and the fulfillment of a call to ministry He placed in our lives. We were clueless
about how things were about to unfold but He lovingly prepared the
way for the journey ahead.

First, God led us to a small church that accepted and welcomed
us into their congregation. Then He literally sat us down for about six
months. Bob's a gifted soundman and I am a musician and speaker.
Although our talents should be used for God's glory, sometimes He
says, *"Be still"* in an effort to bring much-needed healing and refresh-
ing. This time of quiet fellowship with the Lord proved to be a blessing because our lives were about to turn very busy. The pastor and his
wife needed help and saw our eagerness to serve. Before long, I was
asked to play the piano and lead worship and Bob was put to work
in the sound room.

Prior to getting married, I had gone to work for a cellular company. Within one year, my salary doubled and I received a promo-
tion. Bob owned a heating, air, and electrical company that God
continued to grow and bless. In every area of our lives we saw the
Lord's favor, blessings, and benefits, all because we chose to walk in
obedience.

My overall health improved tremendously. I continued to suffer with occasional urinary, bladder, and kidney problems but every
time I felt the onset of an infection, we prayed together and claimed
the healing scriptures. With each attack, God miraculously came
through.

The one struggle I could not overcome was dealing with constant
pain where the tumor had been removed. I refused prescription pain
medication but continued praying the healing scriptures every day,

however, I knew why our prayers were not answered. I secretly lived with fear and an increasing anxiety cancer had returned. Desperate for relief, I called and made a doctor's appointment.

Because of my refusal for further treatment after surgery and the *cancer facts,* I dreaded going to the doctor, but we felt it was the wise thing to do. After the examination, he stated the pain could be a result of scar tissue or reoccurring cancer. The only way to know for sure meant another surgery to remove and test the tissue. Fear and panic immediately took hold of my heart. Things were going so good, I quietly wondered if the hammer was about to come crashing down.

Fear is a stronghold Satan uses to torment God's children, and it is important to understand faith *exits* when we open the door to fear. They will not keep company with each other because faith is light and fear is darkness. The Bible tells us light has *nothing* to do with darkness.

Job always seems to come to our minds when we think about suffering because of what he endured. He proved to be a righteous, God fearing, and faithful servant of the Most High God; however, *the very thing he feared and dreaded had come upon him.*

> What I feared has come upon me; what I dreaded has happened to me. I have no peace, no quietness; I have no rest, but only turmoil.
>
> (Job 3:25, 26 NIV)

Doubts and fears will come into our minds, but we must learn to immediately speak the *Truth* and cast them out. The Word tells us to *"Cast down imaginations and anything which exalts itself above God."* The New International Version translates *"cast down"* as demolish. I love this translation because it brings clarity to what I must do according to scripture. To demolish means, "to completely and utterly destroy!"

The following scriptures give us the authority in Jesus name to refuse any negative report about our life that is contrary to the Word. We can cast it down and speak life, while waiting with expectancy for Jesus to come through.

> For though we live in this world, we do not wage war as the world does. The weapons we fight with are not the weapons of the world. On the contrary, they have divine power to *demolish* strongholds. We *demolish* arguments and every pretension that sets itself up against the knowledge of God, and *we take captive every thought to make it obedient to Christ.*
>
> (2 Corinthians 10:3–5 NIV, emphasis added)

Let me give you an example on how to speak *God's Truth* to a lie. If you have been told nothing good can ever come of your life, do not believe that lie. Your Father in heaven says when you repent of your sins He will forgive, restore, bless, and prosper you. Find scriptures that apply to your situation, speak them out in faith, and refuse to allow the lies of the enemy to cause lingering doubts or fears. If you secretly have unbelief and fear hidden in your heart, repent and continue speaking forth His Word, regardless of the circumstances.

As test and trials come, we must remember whatever happens in our life has gone through the *Father filter.* Other words, He has okayed it for a reason. It is up to us to seek His face and trust Him. If we allow Him to work in our lives these difficulties will bring us into a closer relationship with the Lord, as He *"works out all things for the good."*

God allowed Job to be tested and he withstood the test. Because of this, the Father rewarded his faithfulness. In fact, he got *double* for his trouble! Job 42:10 *says, "After Job had prayed for his friends, the Lord made him prosperous again and gave him **twice** as much as he had before."* What God did for Job He will do for all who faithfully believe and stand firm!

> For God hath not given us the spirit of fear; but of power, and of love, and of a sound mind.
>
> (2 Timothy 1:7 KJV)

> There is no fear in love. But perfect love drives out fear, because fear has to do with punishment. The one who fears is not made perfect in love.
>
> (1 John 4:18 NIV)

The day of surgery came and Bob stayed close by in constant prayer. A praying spouse is a powerful and wonderful thing. The scar tissue was removed and tested. No cancer could be found, praise God for victory!

The doctor advised us to give it a few weeks and the pain should be gone. Three, four, then eight weeks passed, instead of the pain leaving it intensified. In fact, it was actually worse than it had ever been. Panicked, I hit my knees, *"What is going on God? There is no cancer and they got the scar tissue, so why am I having this pain?"*

Desperation can be a wonderful thing; it causes us to take giant steps toward God with a willingness to learn. Of course, the Lord knows this and it is probably why He allows certain obstacles to come our way. He knows what it will take to get our complete and undivided attention!

In the midst of the struggle, we felt the Lord leading us to pray and fast about not only the pain, but also our faith walk. Daily Bible reading and meditating had become a priority, but we found ourselves longing for a more intimate relationship with the Lord. As our hunger grew, we found regular church services no longer satisfied our desire for more of God.

We began listening to a minister on television who taught a series on prayer and fasting. We scanned the channels and found a few other teachers and preachers we enjoyed learning from as well. A new confidence and strength emerged from this time we spent together with God.

One thing became very clear early on; we had to stop tolerating things in our lives that did not line up with an overcoming life. It is quite liberating when you decide to stop putting up with the enemy's lies and attacks; however, once you make this commitment be prepared for spiritual warfare. Satan does not take kindly to losing his edge. The fear I once secretly tucked away had been replaced with faith, and we were now a powerful force because *there is strength in numbers.* The Lord was teaching us the importance of coming into total agreement with Him.

Halfway through the fast, I quickly noticed an entire day passed without pain. The next day came and went, still no pain. The enemy tried to tell me the relief was only temporary. Every time those thoughts entered my mind, *I completely and utterly destroyed them by speaking healing scriptures with authority in the name of Jesus.* The fourth and fifth day passed, still no pain—it was gone!

The evening of the fifth day, I finally told Bob. I explained how fear tried to creep in and that is why I waited to tell him. After a year of constant pain and suffering, I was healed! We sat crying and praising God for answered prayer. We realized once our hearts and mouths lined up with *Truth* and our complete trust rested in the Lord, the miraculous manifested.

From the very beginning, God desired to heal me completely. Unfortunately, I allowed circumstances and pain to get me off track. Without realizing it, my faith hinged on the doctor's assurance cancer no longer existed. God allowed me to receive this confirmation through surgery in order to get to the heart of the matter, fear and a lack of trust in Him.

We are thankful for this experience because we gained an understanding on how powerful the Word is when your heart and mouth get into agreement. The anointing that breaks yokes and delivers miracles comes as we *speak* in faith and *apply* the Word to our lives.

Even though pain and fear persisted, every day I faithfully read and meditated on healing scriptures. I personalized the scriptures by putting my name in them, *"By His stripes I, (Donna Wilcox) am healed."* God did not ignore my persistence, and it became a vital key to receiving a miracle.

If you are doing this already and still have not received an answer, ask the Holy Spirit to reveal any areas of unforgiveness, fear, doubt, or sin. After you have done all you know to do, stand firm, keep a heart (and mouth) of praise, and expect a miracle!

See yourself well with the eyes of the Spirit. Do not allow circumstances and flesh to blur your vision. God works in the spirit realm, the supernatural. Your miracle is already complete in the Spirit; with a heart of praise and anticipation wait on the Father to manifest it in the natural. Man's impossibilities are God's possibilities. *"Jesus looked at them and said, with man this is impossible, but with God all things are possible"* (Matthew 19:26 NIV).

Since that week of prayer and fasting I have not suffered with neck pain in the surgery area and I am completely cancer-free! The miracle of my healing has touched many lives and we cannot stop praising God for His goodness. I make it a point to share my testimony every opportunity I get, and I love it when people see the scars and are willing to ask, *"Hey, did you have a car accident or something?"* Sharing the miracle working power of God is such a privilege. The lessons we learned and the long road to recovery continue to serve a tremendous purpose in seeing others receive miracles, and encouraging them to *fall* into a lifelong trust relationship with the Father.

> Praise the Lord, O my soul; all my inmost being, praise His holy name. Praise the Lord, O my soul, and forget not all His benefits—who forgives all your sins and heals all your disease, who redeems your life from the pit and crowns you with love and compassion, who satisfies your desires with good things so that your youth is renewed like the eagles.
>
> (Psalm 103:1–5 NIV)

God not only healed me of cancer and constant pain, He also restored my youth just like the scripture promises, *"who satisfies your desires with good things so that your youth is renewed like the eagles."*

Before Mother went home to heaven, she prophesied that God planned to do this very thing. One night while we sat talking and laughing she looked at me and stated, *"Donna, you spent your entire young life in pain and the Lord is going to restore those years. You will be youthful and full of life. You are going to do all the things you never got to do when you were growing up."*

God stayed true to His Word and gloriously fulfilled this promise. I cannot help but feel a little sorry for Bob, I am sure there are times he feels like he married a teenager. The beauty of it is the fact he knows my past and how Satan robbed me of so much, but praise God I am making up for it now!

Bob has expanded my horizons in many fun and exciting ways; he taught me how to snow ski and go four wheeling, but more importantly, we share Jesus together around the world. I have energy and enjoy life to its fullest, without the fear of sickness, disease, or constant pain. *Life is good and it is all because of Jesus!*

The Lord continued to work His supernatural magic as He orchestrated the next move. The youth pastor at our church resigned and only a handful still attended class. The pastor's wife asked us to step in and we hesitantly said yes, even though we quietly prayed for a way out. Seeing so much rebellion in young people caused us to want to pull back and avoid working with them. The fact is, we did something awful and pre-judged those precious lives. God soon convicted us of our rush to judgment and we asked for forgiveness. As we stepped out in obedience, His blessings poured down!

Jesus spent His life *serving*, and He left us a beautiful example of compassionate servanthood that we are to continue today. Too often, we are full of excuses as to why we cannot help others, such as *we did not receive a direct word from the Lord*. It is time to wake up and realize that God should not have to speak in an *audible voice* before we are willing to contribute our time and talents. If we expect the Father to be faithful, shouldn't we be faithful too? A *heart of compassion* and *servant driven* must be a huge part of who we are in Christ.

> I tell you the truth, whatever you did for one of the least of
> these brothers of Mine, you did for Me.
> (Matthew 25:40 NIV)

Please do not misunderstand what I am trying to convey. Volunteering for everything under the sun will cause us to lose balance and harmony in our own lives, creating disorder and neglect. We must take care of what God has already entrusted us with, such as our families. Sometimes *"no"* is the right answer. When *"no"* is necessary, this can give someone else the opportunity to reap blessings from their obedience.

Bob and I sought God for wisdom in dealing with the youth group and something interesting happened. One of the new girls with a limited knowledge of church or the Bible began asking questions. Her inquisitive nature became contagious, and the kids who were raised in church started asking questions as well. We were surprised at how little they knew about the Bible. It did not take but a few questions to realize just how ignorant we were too. Don't you hate it when you look stupid in front of a bunch of teenagers! We should have known the answers to their questions. They were hungry and needed spiritual food.

We knew healing scriptures, but that was not enough. Feeling a strong conviction and burden for these kids, a deeper desire to grow more radical in serving the Lord in *Spirit* and *Truth* burned within our hearts. This could mean the difference in where they spent eternity, and we were accountable to them and God.

As our relationship with the young people flourished we made a discovery—the ones who had been raised in church with parents in active ministry were not seeing God's Word put into practice in their own homes. This made us take serious inventory of our lives with a determination to change. Some of them continued to refuse to accept Jesus as their Savior because they did not believe anyone *truly* lived a Christian life. They did not want what the church had to offer. As far as they were concerned, we were all a bunch of hypocrites. You know what, they weren't too far off base.

Committing the situation to prayer, we came up with this simple answer, *"Don't just talk it, but live it. Avoid being just another social hangout. Teach them the Word of God without a lot of fluff or pretense, and love them unconditionally."* In our heart of hearts, we knew if these young people would fall in love with Jesus they would quit looking at everyone else and start getting their own life right. With prayer and fasting, we put our plan in motion.

We began teaching salvation and the very basics of Christianity, then slowly moved into more of God's Word. As they soaked it in, the atmosphere changed. We were having the time of our life and you could feel the very presence of the Holy Spirit. They continued to ask questions and we all grew and learned together.

Some of them were going through difficult situations at home and came to live with us for a period of time. They learned to trust us and realized, living a Christian life is possible inside and outside the church. We felt like proud and protective parents, constantly thanking God for our growing family.

Through this experience, the Father gloriously fulfilled a void in my heart. It allowed me the privilege of loving, mothering, and pampering these kids. He did not just give me one child, He gave me a whole youth group. Isn't that just like God to give us more than we ever dared to dream or imagine!

The Father also knew Bob and I needed growth in every area of our walk, not just in faith and healing matters. To accomplish this He made us accountable to a bunch of young people who were not afraid to ask the hard questions and expect answers. His ways are mysterious and wonderful!

God was moving mightily within our group. Young people were literally coming in off the streets and receiving Jesus as their Savior during our services. The kids were so on fire for God we even set aside an additional night just for prayer. Our dreams and desires for them were manifesting right before our very eyes. Just when things were going great, the enemy reared his ugly head and launched an attack.

One Sunday morning as I played the piano, the entire youth group came up to the choir singing and worshiping the Lord. Suddenly they moved out into the congregation and began praying for people. This had been a dream of ours—to see the youth worshiping like this in our regular services and reaching out to others in prayer. Crying so hard I could hardly play, I glanced back at Bob in the sound room. I could see tears in his eyes and a strange look on his face. I did not give it much thought, figuring he just felt overwhelmed with how God was answering our prayers.

When we got in the car to go home he looked at me and said God spoke to him during the worship. Excited and sure it was something good, his expression said otherwise. He stated God said our time there was done. I could not believe it and began to cry, *"What do you mean, done? These are our kids and I love them. We can't leave them now that they are just beginning to fall in love with Jesus!"* I knew how much Bob loved them too. He tried to comfort me, but the word of the Lord had been very clear. I also knew he never said things like, *"God spoke"* unless He truly did.

Within days our congregation began to unravel. The enemy attacked without mercy, using church people to bring about the chaos. He tried to destroy all the good God had accomplished. Many people were uncomfortable with the street kids wandering into the congregation who were "not churched." We could not believe our eyes and ears—weren't we to win the lost to Christ? The Lord quickly reminded us of what He had spoken to Bob just a week earlier. We had been obedient with everything He asked us to do, and now it was out of our hands.

The young people were devastated as they watched things unfold. When we told them the Lord said our time there was done, their hearts were broken. We had become a very special family. We prayed for God to protect their hearts and minds, and bring people into their lives who would continue sowing *Truth* and *love*.

Scriptures tell us there will be persecution and trouble, but God will deliver us from them all. He also promises not to put more on us than we can bear. I truly do not believe our hearts could have taken any more pain and heartache. In prayer, we committed the situation and those precious lives back to Him.

It may be eternity before we see the fruit of our labor, but God will complete it and bring glory to His kingdom. Whatever you are doing for the Lord, *"don't become weary in well doing."* Stay obedient and leave the results to God!

In time, some of the young people strayed away, but we knew beyond a shadow of a doubt God's Word had been planted in their hearts. They know what to do to get back on track. This knowledge brings us a lot of comfort.

Conflict is never easy but it can be a great teacher. The entire situation proved to be a valuable stepping-stone, preparing the way for a life in ministry and the importance of how Christ *"learned obedience from what He suffered."*

The straight and narrow may not be an easy road but it is well worth it, and we were pressing forward.

CHAPTER 20

What Will It Cost

Over the next year, we witnessed God's restoration power and many changes. A new corporation bought out the cellular company I worked for which resulted in a huge pay cut. No worries, God's *good* plans for our lives continued to manifest. A major corporation in town offered me a position in one of their call centers, with double the salary plus commission. There is truly no way to out-give God.

My new job opened many doors of opportunity to testify about Jesus' power to heal the sick and restore the broken. I also met other Christians in the workplace and together we became an army for the Lord, claiming the call center as our mission field. God's amazing grace sprung into action as we witnessed salvation and miracles, right there in Corporate America! I am so grateful for the friends God blessed me with during that time. They continue to be a blessing and encouragement in our lives today.

Financially things were booming, so we purchased property with plans to build a house. God blessed Bob with many talents, especially in the area of construction. He built our home and within nine months, we moved in.

Before putting up the sheet rock, I wrote scriptures of healing and blessings on the walls, floors, and above the doors. Around our pool, I wrote scriptures of protection and joy. The Word of God literally surrounded us in every room of the house and throughout the entire property. People often commented on the peace they felt when visiting our home.

Along with the excitement of a home and new beginning, came a strength and attitude of praise that continued to reap a harvest of peace and blessings. We were learning the joy and rest that comes from placing our complete trust in Christ.

> And hope does not disappoint us, because God has poured out His love into our hearts by the Holy Spirit, whom He has given us.
>
> (Romans 5:5 NIV)

During this transition period, God directed us to "The Harbor" in Holley, only fifteen minutes from our new home. The Pastor, Greg Coleman, and his family were long time friends; in fact, they produced the album I recorded years earlier. Greg's musical talents and abilities, as well as Mark and Kim's, (his brother and sister-in-law) are known around the country and they have recorded for numerous Christian artists. Pastor Greg's motto was, *"Our mission is fishing!"* We truly appreciated his faithful support and his heart for the lost was an inspiration.

Once again, the Lord took us to a *quiet place* of rest as He prepared to move us up to another level in our Christian walk. One of my heart's desires was to be healed of hand tremors and blood pressure problems without taking pills every day, but several physicians advised me I would suffer a chemical imbalance and other physical complications without the medications.

Doctors and medicines are not sinful or wrong; however, throughout the years my dependence on their abilities instead of God's power to heal remained a huge stronghold. This victory was going to cost my flesh something, but if I held on to the Word and trusted God, the benefits would outweigh the sacrifice.

Unfortunately, flesh had ruled my life for a very long time in this area, therefore bringing it under submission to the Spirit of the Living God that dwelled within me would not be easy. Regardless of the difficulties, I purposed in my heart not to cave in under pressure.

Satan quickly attacked by replaying the many years I spent in a fog of confusion with constant tremors and severe headaches. Tired of the enemies annoying attempts to dampen my faith I decided to show him a thing or two, so I went off the medication cold turkey.

I made the mistake of presuming since God healed me of cancer everything else would be a piece of cake . . . a walk in the park. Yes, this is a cliché, but it best describes my state of mind!

It was not long before my head began pounding and my mind felt like it had short-circuited. I sat in my glider rocking back and forth, yelling out healing scriptures like a crazy woman. Thank heavens no one was peering through the window at that moment!

Bob soon came to my rescue and made a powerful suggestion by saying, *"Baby, maybe your faith is not big enough just yet to go cold turkey. It needs to grow. Why don't you take half now and as your faith grows, steadily decrease the medication."* WOW, what an awesome revelation; I needed to keep growing my faith!

This lesson continues to ring true today. We must never stop growing in the Word and faith, regardless of what we have overcome by the grace of God and the blood of the Lamb. Yesterday's victories will not sustain us. It is vital to keep the soil fed and regularly watered.

Listening to Bob's wise counsel, I cut the dosage in half and set out on a new and deeper *"faith growing"* project. Within a month, I was off the medication altogether. Victory at last!

A few weeks later, I came home with a blinding headache. I knew I had been delivered, but the pain would not go away. Bob suggested I go upstairs, get alone with God, and just spend time praising Him. Immediately, I felt this was the right thing to do.

Lying across the bed in one of our guest rooms, I starting singing praises and worshipping God for all He had done. I thanked Him for everything I could think of and rejoiced in His power of restoration in our lives. In the midst of praying, God gave me a vision of a broken television. In bold letters on the front was the name of the manufacturer. In one of the most humbling moments of my life I heard, *"Donna, if you tried everything and could not fix this TV, what would you do?"* I immediately responded, *"I would call the maker of the television."* After I spoke those words, I heard the Lord say, *"I created you, I will fix you, but will you trust Me?"* Sensing victory close at hand, I quickly responded with, *"Yes Lord, I trust You!"*

Although the pain continued for a few more hours, a spirit of joy burst forth like a fountain as I enjoyed a sweet and glorious time of fellowship with the Father. These lessons in praise and trust have become a treasured gift, and I am praying all who read this discovers its power!

When we are in battle and spiritual warfare, praise is one of the greatest weapons we have at our disposal. With authority in Jesus Christ, we should remind Satan of the *Truth*, even if we have to speak it in fear and trembling. In our weakness, God will be our strength. I heard a minister on television make this statement, *"Instead of telling God how big your problems are, tell your problems how big your God is!"* In the middle of the battle, this is something we must remember to do without hesitation or delay.

God continued to teach us the importance of a growing faith. Every time I grew anxious because of something a doctor said I gave it to the Lord. One day I came across a scripture that put everything in perspective, *"Stop trusting in man, who has but a breath in his nostrils. Of what account is he?"* (Isaiah 2:22 NIV)

Miraculous victories manifest when we are tested, tried, and matured. Only then will we develop the kind of faith that says, *"Be it unto me according to Thy Word."* The kind of faith that continually praises God in thanksgiving, as it waits and rest in *His* ability and *His* power to hear and answer our prayers.

> You dear children are from God and have overcome them, because the One who is in you is greater than the one who is in the world.
>
> (1 John 4:4 NIV)

> Consider it pure joy, my brothers, whenever you face trials of many kinds, because you know that the testing of your faith develops perseverance. Perseverance must finish its work so that you may be mature and complete, *not lacking anything!*
>
> (James 1:2–4 NIV, emphasis added)

Feeling victorious and a little wiser, I decided to go into battle again. This time I sought God for deliverance from monthly hormone shots. The recommended pills did not absorb properly in my system, so for years I had been receiving injections. Concerned about the dangerous side affects, I prayed for another miracle.

If you suffer with hot flashes, you can truly appreciate the benefits of hormone therapy; however, there is a down side to the treatment. Science has found a direct link to cancer caused by these drugs, and I believe I am a prime example of this very fact. When I lived in New York, my doctor discovered that over a ten-year period I had been prescribed 40 milligrams of hormone a month when it should have only been 10! Every time I received an injection, it threw me into a sick headache with nausea and vomiting. I complained, but continued to be told it was the result of receiving the hormone by shot, nothing could be done except control the symptoms with pain and nausea medications. Later, when I was diagnosed with cancer, doctors speculated this might have played a big part in the disease.

It is vitally important for us to educate ourselves and seek wisdom about anything we allow in our temple, because the Word says our bodies are the "Temple of the Lord!"

Under the supervision of a doctor, I stopped taking the shots and began experimenting with natural herbs and vitamins that balance mood swings, reduce hot flashes, and build up the immune system. Exercise and a good diet also became a daily part of my life (not just occasionally). I consistently began treating my temple in a way that pleased God, and His blessings manifested physically, emotionally, and spiritually. I was healthier than I had ever been.

Any victory in this life will cost us something. If we dig in and answer the call to move up higher in God, it will be worth it. I have said this before and I pray it gets down deep in your spirit, "*Father God does not show favoritism.*" Jesus Christ will do the same for you as He did for me. He longs to bring healing and deliverance to *all* who seek Him in faith, refusing to waver in doubt and unbelief. In and through Him, the weak is made strong, the poor is made rich, and the sick is made well!

There is a story in the Bible the Holy Spirit brought to my attention regarding King David. According to 1 Chronicles 21: 1, Satan incited David to take a census of Israel. David then ordered Joab and his army commanders to take a military census of all his fighting men. This action perhaps was a source of pride, turning David's focus away from the Lord. God wanted David to count on and boast in His strengths and abilities alone, not in the strength of his men.

> David was conscience-stricken after he had counted the fighting men, and he said to the Lord, I have sinned greatly in what I have done. Now, O Lord, I beg You, take away the guilt of Your servant. I have done a very foolish thing.
>
> (2 Samuel 24:10 NIV)

The Lord spoke to David through Gad, the prophet. He gave him three options and told David to choose one to be carried out against him. The options were three years of famine, three months of fleeing his enemies while they pursued him, or three days of plague in the land. David thought it over and made his decision.

> David said to Gad, "I am in deep distress. Let us fall into the hands of the Lord, for His mercy is great; but do not let me fall into the hands of men.
>
> (2 Samuel 24:14 NIV)

The Lord sent a plague on Israel for the designated time. David cried out to God to spare his people and only punish him and his family. The Bible says the angel stretched out his hand to destroy Jerusalem and the Lord was grieved. He told the angel, *"Enough! Withdraw your hand."* When the angel withdrew, it was at the threshing floor of Araunah the Jebusite. Gad told David to build an altar to the Lord on the threshing floor of Araunah, so David went up as he was commanded. When Araunah saw him coming he went out, bowed to him, and said; *"Why has my Lord the king come to his servant."* David advised Araunah he came to buy the threshing floor to build an altar to the Lord, so that the plague on the people would cease. Araunah wanted to give it to David without charge.

Meditate on the following scripture and allow what David said to penetrate your spirit with insight and wisdom.

> But the king replied to Araunah, "No, I insist on paying you for it, I will not sacrifice to the Lord my God burnt offerings *that cost me nothing.*"
>
> (2 Samuel 2:24 NIV, emphasis added)

There are numerous lessons to be learned from this story, but take a moment and focus on two important things David said:

1. He requested to fall into God's hands of mercy not the hands of men, *"Let us fall into the hands of the Lord, for His mercy is great."*

2. David realized that God is worthy of our sacrifices and it *should* cost something. *"I will not sacrifice to the Lord my God burnt offerings that cost me nothing."*

Whether we are being tested or growing our faith, the choice to *fall* into a trust relationship with God and allow Him to mold us into His image and likeness, *will* cost us something. However, we can rest in the fact He is merciful, just, and full of goodness.

As Bob and I continued to be tested, we stood in awe of the blessings and benefits we reaped from our obedience and desired to see more of the power of God demonstrated in our lives. We purposed to stay armed and ready for whatever came our way, but had no idea the many rewards from *"staying the course"* the next few challenges would render.

CHAPTER 21

How Bad Do You Want It?

Jesus Christ can break the generational curses in our lives when we commit our will to Him and determine to stay obedient, regardless of circumstances or what we perceive it will cost. It boils down to this one question: *"How bad do you want it?"*

I continued to deal with occasional bladder and kidney infections, which caused frustration and a lot of discomfort. God always came through, but I was weary from the attacks. Deciding I had tolerated this problem long enough, the next request on my list was complete deliverance and healing.

Experiencing these kinds of victories require sacrifice and soul searching, so we took the matter before the Lord and prayed for a total internal makeover! The road ahead would not be easy.

First, we looked at the medical facts: 1) A small urethra; 2) Bladder and kidney problems passed down through generations on my mother's side; 3) Scarring on my left kidney caused by the diseased spleen. We gave these facts to God and prayed for wisdom on how to proceed.

> *Trust in the Lord* with all your heart and lean not on your own understanding; In all your ways acknowledge Him, and He will make your paths straight. Do not be wise in your own eyes; fear the Lord and shun evil. *This will bring health to your body and nourishment to your bones.*
>
> (Proverbs 3:5–8 NIV, emphasis added)

We began the process by looking at our life through a spiritual microscope. No matter how insignificant, we searched for anything that might hinder our prayers from being answered. Within just a few days, Bob made an unwanted observation and lovingly brought it to my attention.

Every morning before leaving for work, I grabbed a Coca-Cola as I headed out the door. In fact, I always had a Coke nearby, and anyone with kidney or bladder problems knows soft drinks are frowned upon. When Bob pointed this out, I quickly presented a good argument stating I never drank but a few sips. Usually the same Coke I left with in the morning stayed in my car and at the end of the day I poured out what remained. While this statement held *fragments* of the truth, I failed to *"fess up"* to everything. I usually drank several cokes throughout the day. Sad to say, but anyone around me for very long knew three things; I never went anywhere without perfume and lipstick, and *I loved Coca-Cola!*

As I continued sounding off my defense Bob looked me in the eyes asking a simple but powerful question, *"Baby, how bad do you want it?"* An alarm went off in my brain. Why did I become so defensive over something as ridiculous as a Coke? Realizing I needed deliverance from this crutch and addiction, I decided to go on a one week fast from my beloved soft drink. Doing without food was not difficult for me, but giving up Coke meant *serious business!*

To some, this may seem small and ludicrous, but it is *"the little foxes that ruin the vineyards."*

> Catch for us the foxes, the little foxes that ruin the vineyards
>
> (Song of Songs 2:15, NIV)

Growing up, I remember typing sermon notes for my Dad on the *"little foxes"* in our lives. I never fully understood his message until that moment. When we give God permission to prune and cut away things that hinders or hurts our lives (spiritually, emotionally, or physically), He shines a spotlight on every area that keeps us from becoming and accomplishing everything He has prepared. He longs for His sons and daughters to be fully equipped, powerful, and *"lacking no good thing."* Throughout the process, we have the choice to

take heed and obey or ignore His instructions and suffer the consequences. *Our decision determines and reveals how bad we really want it!*

You may wonder why I did not stop drinking Cokes years earlier.
Short and simple, my flesh ruled. Before you pass judgment, allow
me to point out a few *"little foxes"* that may be spoiling your vine.
Ask yourself the following questions and keep in mind, God already
knows the answers.

> What *consumes* your life to the point you *refuse* to do with-
> out it, regardless of what it cost your spirit, health, family,
> church, friends, finances, or emotional stability?

> Are you praying for God's help in an area of your life, yet
> are unwilling to help yourself due to a lack of self-control,
> discipline, or slothfulness (laziness)?

> Do *you say* you want to pray and read your Bible more but
> cannot find time, yet you always have time for your favorite
> sports or television shows? Ouch!

> Could you turn your television off for a week or even a day,
> and use that time to fellowship with God and your family
> with a *Christian* and *joyful* attitude?

> What would you have to give up in order to set aside 30
> minutes (or an hour) each day in prayer, Bible reading, and
> communing with God? And, just as important, are you
> willing to do it?

> Do you pray for God to help you with a weakness or addic-
> tion, yet continue to hang out with old friends or acquain-
> tances who participate in those same activities?

Are you defensive, using excuses and tolerating negative things in
your life that are clearly not God's best for you and contrary to the
Truth in His Word? An example of popular excuses:

God made me this way; surely He does not expect me to change.

So and so hurt me, and it was not my fault. Because of them, I am a victim and will have to live like one for the rest of my life.

I am just like my mother/father; everyone knows you cannot fight heredity.

These are all lies and traps of Satan. They are devised to destroy and quench the Spirit of the Living God from breathing *life* and *Truth* into our situations.

Take inventory today. As you meditate on these things, ask the Holy Spirit to reveal the *"little foxes"* in your life. Stop allowing the enemy's lies to hinder your prayers. Although it is painful, give the Holy Spirit permission to prune these destructive branches away, and when Satan tries to bring them back . . . *Resist and draw near to God.* You will be amazed at the fruit just waiting to burst forth. *Your life will never be the same; it will be worth it all!*

After one week of no Cokes, my spirit felt strong and victorious. I determined to change and do whatever it took to walk in divine health. Before long, the issue no longer held me captive and I learned the importance of moderation. It is a beautiful thing!

Our bodies are the *"Temple of the Lord"* and we control what enters them. My bladder and kidneys simply responded to the law of sowing and reaping, producing infections. Although Coke was not the only culprit, it had the strongest hold on me.

Through this experience and willingness to be obedient, the Holy Spirit began revealing other hindrances in the healing process and I made the necessary changes. I purposed to use wisdom in all matters pertaining to my spiritual, emotional, and physical well-being. Am I always successful? No. However, I no longer tolerate and allow negative and damaging things to take up residence as I once did!

> Everything is permissible—but not everything is beneficial. Everything is permissible—but not everything is constructive.
>
> (1 Corinthians 10:23 NIV)

In this scripture Paul was talking about a Believer's freedom. Although we can apply it to many things in our lives, I found it particularly appropriate in reference to the Coca-Cola situation. Just because it is permissible does not make it beneficial. Many times people scolded me about drinking soft drinks, knowing the effects it could have on my bladder and kidneys. I am sure they were not the least bit surprised when I continued to have problems and my prayers were not answered.

There are other issues in society people have varying opinions about, like drinking. Alcoholism in America is one of the main contributors to abuse, death, and divorce. Knowing the adverse and devastating affects of alcohol, Christians should be exceptionally careful. We must love others enough to lay down our rights; even if we do not feel it is wrong. If a friend or acquaintance does not believe in drinking, do not invite them to your home and serve wine. It is just that simple. Bob's father was an alcoholic; therefore, his views on the subject are from experience. He has seen how lives can be touched and torn apart by addiction and abuse.

Being raised in a minister's home, I can recall countless times Dad had to go out all hours of the night to deal with a situation involving alcohol related incidents. It is truly heartbreaking. As Believers, we must be keenly aware of the impact our Christian walk has on those around us. Knowing this, Paul goes on and instructs us to be careful not to judge one another by what is right or wrong according to our conscience; and admonishes us *not to* cause anyone to stumble by what we say or do. The Bible does not always state "such and such" is a sin; however, if it is going to cause harm to your temple or create a stumbling block for anyone, we obviously should *not* do it!

Food is another area of concern. Statistics show obesity is at an all time high in America. We should practice moderation and balance in the things we eat. Exercise must also be a part of our lives. I often hear people complain about how hard they try to lose weight but nothing happens. When the fact of the matter is, they do not exercise or change their eating habits. This kind of behavior reminds me of a famous saying, *"The definition of insanity is doing the same thing over and over and expecting different results" (Benjamin Franklin).* It comes down to this, why should God do something for us when we are not willing to do anything for ourselves? It goes back to that nagging question, *"How bad do you want it?"*

After a time of walking in wisdom and making the necessary changes, infections grew fewer but did not cease. We were dealing with more than Coke; we had to break the bondage of a generational curse and stronghold. This required prayer, fasting, and a determination to hang on until the miraculous manifested.

The Bible talks about blessings and curses handed down from generation to generation. As far back as anyone could remember kidney and bladder problems had been prevalent on Mother's side of the family. This was definitely a curse, and I intended to destroy it once and for all with the bondage breaking power of Jesus Christ.

There are difficult situations in our lives that require intercessory prayer. Someone willing to stand in the gap and pray; someone tenacious and unwilling to give up until victory has arrived. Bob interceded on my behalf and I am forever grateful. When I felt weak in spirit, physically tired, and emotionally drained, he persevered.

There is a wonderful illustration of intercession in the book of Exodus. The Amalekites attacked the Israelites while they were at Rephidim. Moses instructed Joshua to choose some men and go fight.

> As long as Moses help up his hands the Israelites were winning, but whenever he lowered his hands, the Amalekites were winning. When Moses hands grew tired, they took a stone and put it under him and he sat on it. Aaron and Hur held his hands up—one on one side, one on the other—so that his hands remained steady till sunset. Joshua overcame the Amalekites army with sword.
>
> (Exodus 17:11–13 NIV)

Believers will see God move in mighty ways when we allow ourselves to be an "Aaron" or "Hur." I personally desire the *Spirit of Intercession* more in my life, a prayer warrior willing to *stand in the gap* for others. I pray you have this same desire. *God moves powerfully when we reach out in prayer for those in need.*

> Have I not commanded you? Be strong and courageous. Do not be terrified; do not be discouraged, for the Lord your God will be with you wherever you go.
>
> (Joshua 1:9 NIV)

> The righteous cry out, and the Lord hears them; He delivers them from *all* their troubles. The Lord is close to the broken hearted and saves those who are crushed in spirit. A righteous man may have many troubles, but the Lord delivers him from them *all.*
>
> (Psalm 34:17–19 NIV, emphasis added)

CHAPTER 22

The Truth Will Set You Free

> For I know the plans I have for you, declares the Lord,
> plans to prosper you and not to harm you, plans to give you
> hope and a future. Then you will call upon Me and come
> and pray to Me, and I will listen to you. You will seek Me
> and find Me when you seek Me with all your heart. I will be
> found by you, declares the Lord ...
>
> (Jeremiah 29:11–14 NIV)

After one year of enjoying great health, I came down with a serious kidney infection. Feeling confident in the steps I had taken toward walking in wisdom, being good to my body, and reflecting back on all the miracles of healing God had given us, I concluded doctors were no longer necessary in my life. If you have not figured it out by now, I can be an extremist at times. Doing anything halfway usually is not an option.

The very thought of ever going to the doctor again brought feelings of failure and condemnation. This should have been a *big red flag* since I knew the Word clearly tells us, *"Therefore, there is now no condemnation to those who are in Christ Jesus"* (Romans 8:1). When we are burdened with condemnation, it is important to examine our hearts and ask the Holy Spirit to reveal the lie and replace it with God's *Truth*.

With stubborn resistance, a rising temperature, and severe pain I walked around the house everyday praising God and quoting healing scriptures. I knew this kidney infection was nothing for the Almighty Physician compared to what He had already accomplished. I told Bob, *"God's ways are not our ways and I am certain His ways do not include a doctor's visit!"* Bob knew what I had been through with doctors and how stubborn I was because of it. He would not force me to go, so he believed for a miracle and continued in prayer and fasting, knowing nothing is impossible with God.

In my estimation, I just needed to toughen up and hang on. After all, God does not lie, His Word is true, and He is required to do what He says . . . Right? The answer to that question is yes, God will always be faithful to His Word; however, we must humbly seek Him for direction and not use the Bible as a tool in telling Him what He is required to do for us!

At this point, I had lost all rational perspective. The Lord was my Physician and mere man had no right to touch me. Somehow, I envisioned every doctor that crossed my path was cleverly sent by Satan. I just imagined the enemy at work in these unsuspecting men and women causing them to lose all sense of good judgment when I walked into their exams rooms, and proceed to diagnose and prescribe things that would bring about my demise! I realize this sounds a bit paranoid, but because of my past the enemy did not need much help in getting me to arrive at this conclusion.

Going to the doctor does not stop the Lord from performing miracles. When we can do something for ourselves, it is not wrong to do so; however, at this point no man on earth could have convinced me of that. Only God Himself possessed the ability to straighten out my thinking and bring a balance back into my life.

After a week, things deteriorated drastically as I struggled to stand up and the simple act of breathing caused intense pain. I finally turned to Bob and asked him to take me to the emergency room. He immediately put me in the car and away we went.

By the time we arrived my white cell count was over 30,000, (normal is approximately five to seven thousand). After a stern reprimand for letting my condition get so serious, the doctor began an intravenous antibiotic treatment and prepared to admit me into the hospital.

A few days passed and my kidneys were not responding to treatment. The doctor advised Bob the prognosis did not look good and she needed to change my medication to something stronger. Everyone continued in prayer, even people from the call center where I worked interceded on my behalf. They sent cards and letters thanking me for all the times I prayed for them, stating they were happy to return the favor. Their response blessed me beyond words; many of them were not Believers but had witnessed God's favor and power through prayer. I knew it was only a matter of time before they turned their lives over to Jesus.

Knowing our faith firmly rested in the healing power of God, I questioned why I ended up in the hospital and why had I fallen into the hands of men. There simply had to be a reason, but what was the Lord up to and how would He receive the glory in this situation? Although I did not understand, I trusted Him to work things out for the good.

The Lord does not bring sickness or disease upon us, it is contrary to His character and His Word; however, He allows things to happen for a reason. Sometimes it is simply the law of *"sowing and reaping"* and other times it may be a *"Job situation."* Regardless of the *"why"* as God's children our responsibility is to simply trust Him, even if it means trusting without understanding. The key is to not waiver from the *Truth* of God's Word.

Four days passed and the doctor told Bob she needed to see progress within twenty-four hours or things would take a devastating turn. Everyone waited and prayed. Approximately twenty-three hours later my body finally responded to the antibiotics. God's sense of timing is quite interesting!

The doctor ordered a CAT scan and series of x-rays to determine how much damage my kidneys had suffered. The test showed a perfect set of kidneys. Wait just a minute; where was the scarring on my left kidney caused by the spleen? It strangely disappeared, but that is not possible! Remember the scripture, *"Jesus looked at them and said, with man this is impossible, but with God all things are possible"* (Matthew 19:26 NIV).

Praise the Lord we serve an awesome God! He knew I avoided doctors like a plague, and would never agree to a kidney test or x-rays, so *for my good* He allowed this trial as a tool to *expose the truth.* When He healed me of cancer He also healed my kidney! Having this knowledge meant I could stop professing something that was not there. What we speak is critical to every area of our life, and the Father found a way to get the information to my mouth, heart, and mind; cutting away all deception, lies, and double-mindedness. This added an additional testimony to my long list of praises filled with God's powerful blessings and the miraculous. The Father knows I am not shy when it comes to testifying, so getting the information to me was of utmost importance.

What Satan meant for harm, God used to bring glory to His name and *"right thinking"* back into my life. I no longer believe all doctors are under the Devil's control and out to destroy me. I appreciate their contribution and pray for more of them to personally know and believe in the Lord and Savior Jesus Christ.

Let this be a lesson to you who are stubborn, on the extreme side, and slightly dingy at times . . . *There is hope!* God knows just how to get our attention. I am thankful for His steadfast determination to mold me into a vessel capable of doing mighty things for Him. I can offer hope and encouragement to those who are struggling with sickness, pain, and confusion; teaching them about the life changing power of the Living God. This isn't a job, it is a joy!

Through all of this, Bob and I continued to yearn and pray to see the *"greater works"* Christ talked about displayed more in our own lives and within the entire Body of Christ. Our hearts longed to see the *Gifts of the Spirit* actively at work in a greater way, producing lasting fruit for the Kingdom of God.

Blessed beyond our wildest dreams and living the good life, we were no longer satisfied. Our desires changed with each new victory. We wanted more of God and less worldliness, with a longing to *"go into all the world"* and reach the lost with the Good News of Jesus!

Some people go through their entire Christian walk as bottle babies or toddlers. Once the Lord blesses them with "things" (friends, a good job, position in church or community, etc.), they are fully satisfied to stay right there. There is nothing wrong with material blessings and working faithfully in your church and community; however, we must continue yielding Kingdom fruit.

Growing in the Lord and winning souls are an essential part of our daily walk with Christ. A good test to see how we are progressing in our relationship with the Lord is to examine our fruit on a regular basis. Below are a few questions to meditate on during this process:

When is the last time I led someone to Jesus Christ or shared His goodness in my life?

Have I prayed for someone other than myself lately?

Have I walked close enough to God to hear His voice and feel the Holy Spirit urging me to intercede and fast for the lost, sick, or discouraged souls within my church, community, and the world?

When the opportunity arises, am I willing to step out of my comfort zone to obey God?

Am I daily praying, reading the Word of God, and applying what I have learned?

Do I live a life of integrity and excellence in everything I put my hands to, willing to stand up for what is right according to the Bible, regardless of the cost?

Do I continually seek the Holy Spirit to reveal areas in my life that are not pleasing to God as I strive for a closer walk with the Father?

Allow the Holy Spirit to speak to your heart as you meditate on these questions. We all fall short at times, but that should be the *exception* not the *norm*. We should see steady progress and maturity throughout our Christian walk.

You may feel a call to teach a Sunday school class or work with children's church. Regardless of what it is, ask the Holy Spirit to place those students on your heart. Get ready to be awakened in the middle of the night, with no rest in sight until you have hit your knees in prayer for the lives God has entrusted into your hands.

As you go about your daily chores one of those precious faces may come to mind, *stop and intercede* on their behalf. Your ministry will become fruitful, filled with power, and the anointing of the sweet Holy Spirit! You will no longer be *"filling a slot."*

Bob and I felt a shift in our spirits. We sensed an expectancy as God opened doors of opportunity in our new church. Bob was working once again as a soundman and I directed the choir. Forgive me for boasting; but our choir was anointed and filled with hearts seeking hard after God, not to mention beautifully gifted voices! They blessed me more than I ever dreamed possible. Miracles and blessings came about as we lifted our voices in praise and spent time interceding for one another.

A call to full time ministry grew heavy on our hearts. Bob felt directed of the Lord to take the next two years and get all our affairs in order. This meant selling the business and deciding what to do with our home and property. We trusted the Lord to reveal His plans for us within those two years as we continued to *stay the course.*

> Be still and know that I am God; I will be exalted among the nations, I will be exalted in the earth. The Lord Almighty is with us; the God of Jacob is our fortress. Selah.
>
> (Psalm 46:10, 11 NIV)

> Let integrity and uprightness preserve me; for I wait on Thee.
>
> (Psalm 25:21 KJV)

In the midst of the waiting, the Holy Spirit spoke to me about writing my life's story. Filled with questions, I pondered on where and how to begin such an undertaking. I thought, *"How do I put into words all God has done for me? Will people feel His love and presence as they read the pages of my life? Will they be encouraged, or judge me for all the stupid mistakes I have made? Could my life ever truly convey God's unstoppable desire and ability to forgive our sins and restore our lives to something of beauty; all for His glory!"*

The Lord quickly reminded me of the question He asked a year earlier, *"Donna, will you trust me?"* I have never regretted saying *"yes"* as His blessings and miracles literally began overtaking our lives. How could I do anything different now! I promised to be obedient and write the good, the messed up, and the not so pretty, believing for healing and encouragement to flow through the pages to all who read it.

I prayed for God to give me courage and peace about when to tell Bob. We always shared our dreams and thoughts with one another and I did not want to keep this from him, but how do you tell your husband, *"Hey Baby, I am going to write a book!"*

A week passed and Bob came by the office to take me to lunch, as we sat talking in the truck I began spilling everything. I shared with him what I felt the Lord directing me to do and he quickly responded with assurance, encouraging me to be obedient and start writing. Feeling so relieved to have his approval, I wept for joy. When I arrived home from work that day a laptop computer and Bible disk was sitting on the kitchen counter waiting for me.

Nothing is more important to a woman than to have the man she loves display faith and encouragement in the gifts and call God has on her life, while generously surrounding her with love. *I am blessed!*

When we obey, God will pave the way with peace, regardless of our past or the obstacles ahead. His purposes will be accomplished, and His Word will not return void. *Our job is to proceed ahead in faith, and refuse to give in to shame, fear, or disgrace.*

> So is My Word that goes out from My mouth; *it will not return to Me empty; but will accomplish what I desire and*

achieve the purpose for which I sent it. You will go out in joy and be led forth in peace; the mountains and hills will burst into song before you, and all the trees of the field will clap their hands. Instead of the thorn bush will grow the pine tree, and instead of briers the myrtle will grow. This will be for the Lord's renown, for an everlasting sign, which will not be destroyed.

(Isaiah 55:11–13 NIV, emphasis added)

Do not be afraid; you will not suffer shame. Do not fear disgrace; you will not be humiliated. You will forget the shame of your youth and remember no more the reproach of your widowhood. For your Maker is your Husband-the Lord Almighty is His name-the Holy One of Israel is your Redeemer; He is called the God of all the earth. The Lord will call you back as if you were a wife deserted and distressed in spirit-a wife, who married young, only to be rejected, says your God.

(Isaiah 54:4–6 NIV, emphasis added)

CHAPTER 23

Missionary School...Here We Come!

> *Trust* in the Lord, and do good; *Dwell* in the land and
> enjoy safe pasture. *Delight* yourself in the Lord and He will
> give you the desires of your heart. *Commit* your way to the
> Lord; *Trust* in Him, and He will do this; He will make
> your righteousness shine like the dawn, the justice of your
> cause like the noonday sun. *Be still* before the Lord and
> *wait* patiently on Him."
>
> (Psalm 37:3–7 NIV, emphasis added)

I love the outline God gives us in these scriptures to live out our
dreams with His favor and blessings; He says to, trust, dwell, delight,
commit, be still, and wait patiently on Him. Notice *trust* is mentioned twice. After the second *trust*, it states, *"and He will do this; He
will make your righteousness shine like the dawn, the justice of your cause
like the noonday sun."* What a glorious promise, and all because we
choose to *fall into a trust relationship* with the Lord God, our Father!

As we applied these principles, the next chapter of our lives took
us completely out of our comfort zone and into a new dimension of
faith. Within the two years God gave us to get things in order, Bob
sold his business and the call center I worked in closed. Full time
ministry was on its way to becoming a reality! We sent applications
to global ministries and mission organizations and within weeks,
we received a phone call stating we were accepted to a missionary
school in Colorado.

We met with our pastor and asked for his blessings as we stepped
out in faith and began preparation for our new adventure. Our
heart's desires were to sow into young people and encourage them in

their purpose and call in the Kingdom of God while spreading the *Good News* to the world of Christ and His healing power.

During our meeting, Pastor Greg shared a word he received from the Lord when praying for us. He did not know it at the time, but he said the same words my guardian angel spoke in my hospital room when I was nineteen-years-old; *"Many children will pass through your arms and be blessed."* Then Pastor Greg went on to say, *"God will not allow you to leave this world until you fulfill His will and purpose for your life. He has been preparing you both for such a time as this."* Overcome with emotion, Bob and I just looked at each other, unable to utter a word.

Even with these confirmations, we were not without challenges. Before leaving, Polly (my step mom) suffered diabetic complications and went to be with the Lord. Dad seemed to be handling it well, but did not need to be left alone. He had a large four-bedroom home with a swimming pool, too much house for just one person. My niece Amanda, her husband Todd, and two children (Tessa Grace and Sophia Joy) were experiencing some major changes in their lives, so they decided to leave Indiana and move in with Dad in Florida. They too felt called to the mission field so this enabled them to itinerate, raise support, and spend quality time with "Papa." Knowing he would be surrounded by his granddaughter and great-grandchildren gave us a comforting peace about leaving the area.

God continued to beautifully orchestrate His plans and everything seemed to be falling into place. Traci graduated from high school with honors and was accepted to Auburn University in Alabama. This gave Bob peace about leaving, knowing she would soon be setting out on a new adventure all her own.

Two weeks prior to leaving, I came down with a bladder infection. I did not want to go to the doctor but I knew if the symptoms persisted, it was inevitable. We prayed for healing and deliverance, rebuking thoughts of doubt and fear the enemy tried to plant in our minds.

Going into mission's means going to places where hospitals are rare and doctors are not always reliable. The right medications can be hard to come by and it really is a step of faith for someone who has had numerous health issues. Satan desperately tried to get as many punches in as possible in an effort to get our eyes focused on the *"good and comfortable life,"* wanting us to shrink back and change our minds.

His plans failed miserably, instead, it created more of a determination in our hearts to walk the path of obedience and trust God. Bob looked at me and said, *"Baby, maybe we should try something different and go on the offense. Tell the Devil to bring on the symptoms. As he tries to afflict you, purpose to go out and talk to anyone you meet about Jesus. Tell them all the healings and miracles God has given you. We will get him where it hurts!* Then Bob reminded me of Revelations 12:11, *"They overcame him by the blood of the Lamb and the word of their testimony; they did not love their lives so much as to shrink from death."*

I cannot explain it, but my spirit jumped and caused me to go into immediate action when he spoke those words. Fearing the mission field or anything else because of past health issues was no longer an option. At that moment, I realized if I died while telling others about Jesus, at least I would be giving something in return for all He had done for me. God brought me this far, He would victoriously take me all the way!

With that in mind, I got on the phone and called three very dear friends, (Linda, Elaine, and Maxine). I knew they would do anything in the world for me. I asked them if illness ever interfered with my ability to minister, would they hit the streets on my behalf and tell others how Jesus miraculously healed me of cancer (and any other testimony they wanted to share) until I was able to continue the work God called me to do. Without hesitation, they all said YES! After hanging up the phone, I expressed loudly and with authority in Jesus name, *"Devil, the battle lines are drawn."* I advised the enemy to go ahead and bring it on. Not only would I boldly testify for Jesus with every pain and symptom, but my friends were also prepared to go for me ... *Numbers are powerful in the spirit realm!*

We went to bed that night full of determination but I awoke the next morning feeling worse, making me even madder. I dressed, kissed my husband, and headed out the door exclaiming, *"I'm off to witness for Jesus. The Devil must have thought we were kidding."* Bob gave me a big hug as I got in the car and drove away. I immediately felt impressed to go to the hospital and knew it must be God, because it is one of my least favorite things to do in the entire world.

Making a quick detour, I went by a Christian Book Store and bought crosses with the sinner's prayer printed on them and scripture cards filled with God's promises and blessings. Within minutes, I sat in the hospital parking lot telling the Devil just how sorry he would be before the day was over!

I entered the hospital armed with goodies and the *joy of the Lord*. A nurse stopped and asked if she could help me (I must have looked lost). I told her I had some gifts to hand out to anyone who needed someone to talk with, or wanted prayer. She ushered me down the hall to a room and said, *"You can start here. Everyone on this floor could use some encouragement."*

The Holy Spirit prepared the way as I entered each room. The patients were kind and receptive, expressing appreciation for the gifts I left with them. Although most of them did not know Jesus as their Savior, they welcomed prayer and listened as I shared my healing testimony.

Something wonderful happened as I went from room to room praying and testifying about the goodness of the Lord. The pain, burning, and pressure in my bladder and lower back gradually subsided. By the time I finished praying for everyone on that floor the pain had disappeared.

I stepped outside the hospital doors completely healed and feeling victoriously refreshed. As I walked toward the car and passed the emergency room entrance, something inside my spirit said, *"You aren't through yet!"* I was having so much fun messing with the Devil and getting points in for the *"good guys"* that I stopped, backed up, and went in.

A young couple was sitting by the nurse's station and they were quite a remarkable sight. Both of their bodies were tattooed all over with pierced eyebrows, lips, nose, and Lord only knows what else! A normal person might have felt a little afraid or intimidated to strike up a conversation and boldly ask, *"May I pray for you?"* Not me; by this time I felt like I could take on an army.

I sat down next to them and proceeded to testify about how God healed me of cancer, explaining His power to redeem and restore lives. Before I could even finish and with tears in his eyes, this precious young man asked me to pray for his brother. He said something was wrong and the doctors had not been able to figure out the problem. I immediately took their hands and began praying. As I got up to leave, I gave them a cross and scripture card and asked them to read the Bible and keep talking to God. I assured them of His ability to hear and answer prayer. They nodded, thanked me, and shook my hand.

Looking around, I realized the only other people in the emergency room were a little girl and her mother. The child loudly asked, *"Mom, can she pray for me?"* Walking over, I told the young woman I would be happy to pray for her daughter. She seemed a bit reluctant, but the little girl persisted. (I love children)!

I briefly went over my healing testimony again (knowing they overheard most of it already) and asked how I could pray. They were vacationing in Destin at the beach when the little girl came out of the water with red swollen whelps all over her body. I could see red puffy marks on her arms and legs, so I took them by the hands and prayed a simple prayer of faith. I gave them my last cross and scripture card, encouraging them to read their Bibles and discover all the wonderful things about God and His power to heal and bless *all* who believe in Him. I sensed this little girl had faith and believed what I said. Before leaving, she reached up and gave me a great big hug . . . God is so good!

I sat in the parking lot crying tears of joy as I called Bob on the cell phone and shared what God accomplished in those few hours. He was ecstatic! It boosted our faith in such a real and tangible way. We grew even more excited about what the future held, knowing the Father would take good care of us.

Even though we felt we were leaving Florida for good, we did not know if we should rent or sell our home. After praying and seeking the Lord for guidance, we decided to rent it out for the time being and God blessed us with great tenants. With days left to go, countdown began as we sold and gave away the few earthly possessions that remained. Watching as our Wave Runner and little red Corvette pulled out of the driveway without us left me feeling strange and hollow; however, saying goodbye to our dog Blondie was the most devastating task! The school did not allow animals, so we could not take her with us. Thankfully, she went to a loving family in our church.

The day came to leave our house for good and say goodbye. Bob packed every inch of our Chevy Avalanche to capacity. Pulling out in the street, it hit me; we were homeless for the first time in our lives. I started to cry but it quickly turned to laughter when I realized how we must look like the "Beverly Hillbillies" riding down the road. We actually had a rocking chair tied to the bed of the truck! When I regained my composure, a scripture came to mind, *"And everyone who has left houses or brothers or sisters or father or mother or children or fields for My sake will receive a hundred times as much and will inherit eternal life"* (Matthew 19:29 NIV).

We spent a week with Dad before embarking on our new adventure far, far away. The gorgeous beaches that surrounded us would soon be a distant memory. Bob dreamed of one day living in the mountains and we were heading off to the middle of the Sangre de Cristo Mountains, located in beautiful Colorado.

There were several bonuses to living in the mountains. It was much cooler and less humid than Florida. Not to mention, we just happened to love snow skiing. The location put us close to some of our favorite places, with the added privilege of looking out at God's *"purple mountain majesty"* everyday.

After arriving at the mission's base, we saw God move miraculously on our behalf, giving us numerous confirmations about our move. Almost immediately, He began fulfilling the promise He gave me years earlier by adding *spiritual children* to our family from all over the United States, as well as different nations and countries from all around the world. They even referred to me as *"Mama Donna"* and that made my heart deliriously happy!

Our missions work took us to Mexico and eventually to India. Being in these countries opened our eyes to the poverty and pain of so many beautiful people scattered about, trying to survive on the streets, in barrios, slums, and villages. You really cannot comprehend just how extravagant and spoiled we are in America until you spend time working and living among the poor and hurting from other nations.

God used Bob's talents and gifts in construction to build numerous homes for the poor and homeless, a medical clinic in the poverty stricken barrios of Juarez, a three-story leadership school dormitory in Chapala, Mexico, and work place improvements at a candle shop and home (House of Hope) for women and children with HIV/AIDS in India.

The leadership school in Chapala is a place for young missionaries from every nation to come together. They learn techniques and ways to go into the darkest and most unreached places of the world, sharing the hope of Christ and ministering to the needs of people on a practical level.

The clinic we built in Mexico offers medicines and medical attention to those who cannot afford it. Students and professionals from Texas go across the border to volunteer their time and services.

The candle shop in India gives widows, ex-prostitutes, and women with HIV/AIDS a place to learn a trade and make a living for their families. It not only gets them off the streets but also opens the door of discipleship to learn about Jesus and His power to heal and restore broken and hurting lives.

The "House of Hope" offers a home with Christ as its foundation, filled with love, discipleship, instructions on safe and sanitary practical living applications, and medicines for women and children suffering with HIV/AIDS.

The time we spent in the poor areas of Mexico prepared us for what we encountered in India. For several months, we walked to work everyday amongst overwhelming poverty, along with donkeys, cows, pigs, dogs, long-legged goats, water buffalo, cars, and rickshaws. The vast amount of people, animals, pollution, and poverty can astound the most experienced traveler. For us, it was as though the Old Testament had come to life. Idol worship, strange temples, and the chaotic results of a godless confused people surrounded us everyday, but in the midst of it all, we were so grateful to be there.

India was a life changing experience. The people were receptive to learn about Jesus Christ and enthusiastic about understanding the Bible. When I shared my testimony of healing, without hesitation women and children with HIV/AIDS came up requesting prayer to *"this God who heals!"* We witnessed the Father do many amazing and miraculous things, for He truly is a Great and Mighty God!

The women I had the privilege to disciple are my sisters in Christ and they became family in every sense of the word! Leading them in the sinner's prayer and watching their Christian growth inspired and challenged us in so many ways. Some of them faced persecution and trials from family members because of turning from Hinduism to Christianity. It was heart wrenching and hard to accept, yet when they said *"Thank you"* for telling them about the *"One True God"* and expressed the peace and happiness they found from knowing Jesus as their Friend and Savior, it made it all worth it!

The day we left India, our hearts ached. We had established some beautiful friendships and it felt like we were leaving family once again. We purposed to stay obedient and prayed God would lead us back to India in the future, and that continues to be our heart's desire.

> Commit to the Lord whatever you do, and your plans will succeed. The Lord works out everything for His own end.
>
> (Proverbs 16:3, 4a NIV)

I experienced another amazing miracle. During our time in India as well as our extended trips to Mexico, I enjoyed exceptionally good health. In many instances, I experienced fewer problems than those who were younger and had excellent health their entire life. God is faithful and so very good.

My life has felt like a roller coaster at times but what a privilege it is to testify of the goodness of God. Above all, I pray my story has encouraged you to dig deeper and take the plunge. Choose today to *fall* into a *trust relationship* with Jesus Christ as never before! Step out in faith and become the man or woman He longs for you to be. One who is *"lacking no good thing."* Always remember, *nothing is impossible with Father God. He alone has the power to restore the ashes and ruins of any life, making it something of beauty, value, and worth!*

Your greatest weapon against the enemy is to saturate yourself with the Word of God and *by faith* choose to apply what you learn. As you *fall* into your own *trust* relationship with God, your life will be a testimony of His power and goodness to all who see and hear. Get ready for a thrill and enjoy the *f*

a

l

l

!

EPILOGUE

If you are in need of a miracle but are not sure where to begin, start by being honest and getting *"real"* with Jesus today. Make sure you are walking in obedience according to the Word of God. Ask the Holy Spirit to search your heart for anything that might hinder your prayers from being answered. Repent of any unforgiveness, doubt, or sin, and then begin speaking *Truth* to your situation. Find scriptures that relate to what you are praying for and make them personal, boldly speak them out with the authority of Jesus Christ, (Ex: *"By His stripes* I *am healed!"*) Refuse to allow condemnation to sabotage your faith and resist the enemy by drawing near to God.

Guard what goes into your mind, spirit, and body. Great wisdom on how to do this can be found by reading and studying the book of Proverbs. Do not allow your eyes to stay focused on the circumstances; purpose to see through eyes of the Spirit. After you have done this, *wait* and *keep trusting God. Stay the course,* and continue to walk in obedience with the heart of a servant. Keep a *joyful spirit* and remember, *"The joy of the Lord is our strength,"* and *"His strength in made perfect in our weakness."*

> My son, attend to My words; incline thine ear unto My sayings. Let them not depart from thine eyes; keep them in the midst of thine heart. For they are life unto those that find them, and health to all their flesh.
>
> (Proverbs 4:20–22 KJV)

If you do not know Jesus as your personal Savior, please, take a moment and pray a simple prayer that can change your life for eternity!

Before praying, it is important to have an understanding of what you are doing. This prayer is only effective when a person knows, understands, and believes they are a sinner in need of salvation. The Bible clearly tells us we are all sinners, *"As it is written, 'There is none righteous, no, not one"* (Romans 3:10 KJV).

Because of our sins, we deserve eternal punishment (Matthew 25:46). The sinner's prayer is a simple but powerful request for mercy and grace, instead of judgment and wrath (Titus 3:5–7).

The next aspect of a sinner's prayer is to confess that Jesus Christ is the Son of God and that He became flesh, living a sinless and righteous life (2 Corinthians 5:21). Then you must believe Jesus paid the ultimate sacrifice, taking the punishment we deserved by offering Himself and dying on the cross for our sins. On the third day, He victoriously rose from the dead, conquering death, hell, and the grave (1 Corinthians chapter 15). Through this unselfish and loving act of mercy, we can receive forgiveness for our sins with the promise of eternal life in Heaven.

If we receive these *Truths,* we can be saved, but it is only by grace and faith, *"For it is by grace you have been saved, through faith - and this not from yourselves, it is the gift of God"* (Ephesians 2:8 NIV).

Once you have prayed the prayer of salvation, life is not going to turn suddenly blissful, without difficult and frustrating challenges; however, you are a Child of the *Most High God.* He is your Father. Once His Word is applied to your life, blessings will follow. You will enjoy the benefits of peace, joy, love, and so much more!

Sinner's Prayer of Salvation

Dear God, I come before You today in the name of Jesus Christ, Your Son. I believe He died on the cross and shed His blood for the forgiveness of my sins. I believe Jesus rose again from the dead by the power of the Holy Ghost, conquering death, hell, and the grave. Please forgive me of my sins and wash me with Your blood. By faith, I invite You into my heart and life as my personal Savior. Today, I am choosing to follow You for the rest of my life. Help me to walk in Your ways, open my eyes and ears to understand and obey Your Word, and resist everything that is contrary to Your *Truth*. The Bible says You do not show favoritism and You will turn no one away, and that includes me. Thank You for hearing and answering my prayer. I confess and know that I am saved. Jesus, I love You and thank You for saving my soul!

Congratulations and Welcome to the Family of God!

May God Richly Bless You! I am available for seminars, conferences, or speaking engagements. For information, please contact me through my website, http://www.donnawilcox.com

Suggested Reading

God's Plan for Man
By: Rev. Finis Jennings Dake
Dake Bible Sales, Inc

Imprisoned In Iran & A Beautiful Way
By: Dan Baumann
YWAM Publishing

The Tongue–A Creative Force
By: Charles Capps
Harrison House
Tulsa, Oklahoma

Tomorrow You Die
By: Reona Joly
YWAM Publishing

Spiritual Warfare
By: Dean Sherman
YWAM Publishing

Battlefield of the Mind: Winning the Battle in Your Mind
By: Joyce Meyer
Joyce Meyer Trade

The Power of a New Identity
By: Dan Sneed
Sovereign World, Ltd.

Exposing the Lie
By: Dan Sneed
Chosen Books

Good Morning, Holy Spirit
By: Benny Hinn
Nelson Books

Stick a Geranium in Your Hat and Be Happy
Books by Barbara Johnson
W Publishing Group; Bk & Acces edition (October 1994)

Hooked on the Word: Changing Your Life Through Bible Meditation & Dollars, Euros, Pesos
By: Ron Smith
YWAM Publishing

TATE PUBLISHING & *Enterprises*

Tate Publishing is committed to excellence in the publishing industry. Our staff of highly trained professionals, including editors, graphic designers, and marketing personnel, work together to produce the very finest books available. The company reflects the philosophy established by the founders, based on Psalms 68:11,

"THE LORD GAVE THE WORD AND GREAT WAS THE COMPANY OF THOSE WHO PUBLISHED IT."

If you would like further information, please call
1.888.361.9473
or visit our website
www.tatepublishing.com

TATE PUBLISHING & *Enterprises*, LLC
127 E. Trade Center Terrace
Mustang, Oklahoma 73064 USA